28935670

A WOMAN'S WAGE

The Blazer Lectures for 1988

A WOMAN'S WAGE

Historical Meanings and Social Consequences

Alice Kessler-Harris

THE UNIVERSITY PRESS OF KENTUCKY

Copyright © 1990 by Alice Kessler-Harris
Published by The University Press of Kentucky

Scholarly publisher for the Commonwealth,
serving Bellarmine College, Berea College, Centre
College of Kentucky, Eastern Kentucky University,
The Filson Club, Georgetown College, Kentucky
Historical Society, Kentucky State University,
Morehead State University, Murray State University,
Northern Kentucky University, Transylvania University,
University of Kentucky, University of Louisville,
and Western Kentucky University.

Editorial and Sales Offices: Lexington, Kentucky 40506-0336

Library of Congress Cataloging-in-Publication Data

Kessler-Harris, Alice.
  A woman's wage : historical meanings and social consequences /
Alice Kessler-Harris.
    p. cm. — (The Blazer lectures ; 1988)
  Includes bibliographical references.
  ISBN 0-8131-0803-9
  1. Wages—Women—United States—History—20th century. I. Title.
II. Series.
HD6061.2.U6K47 1990
331.4'21'09730904—dc20   89-48812

FOR BERT

Contents

Foreword

The challenge to undertake a fundamental examination and reappraisal of our institutions, culture, and values prompted the establishment of the Blazer Lecture Series. This series, supported since 1949 by the Paul G. and Georgia M. Blazer Fund, has provided students and faculty of the College of Arts and Sciences at the University of Kentucky the opportunity to host a number of distinguished speakers. The generosity of the Blazer family in establishing and renewing this endowment has long benefited the intellectual atmosphere of the college and the surrounding university community by allowing members of that community to participate in the thoughts and ideas being developed by scholars in a number of disciplines.

In the almost four decades since the Blazer Lecture Series was established, the University of Kentucky has been able to present such distinguished speakers as Henry Steele Commager, the noted historian; Barry Bingham, Sr., of the Louisville *Courier Journal*; Henry Cabot Lodge, ambassador and senator; and President Gerald Ford.

The continued generosity and interest of the Blazer family have allowed us in recent years to have as lecturers Dr. William DeVries, noted heart surgeon, and Dr. Daniel Boorstin, Librarian of Congress. In cooperation with the University Press of Kentucky, the College of Arts and Sciences is pleased to be able to share the Blazer Lectures through the publication of an annual monograph.

The 1988 Blazer Lectures were given by Dr. Alice Kessler-Harris at the Lexington campus on April 12 and 13, 1988. The topics of her talks were "The Battle between Equity and Equal-

ity: Historical Perspectives on Justice for Women" and "The
Wage in Context: Gender and the Power to Earn." Dr. Kessler-
Harris, one of the foremost scholars in the nation on women
and work, is professor of history at Temple University. She has
served as chair of the American Historical Association's Committee on Women Historians and as a consultant to the American Civil Liberties Union Women's Rights Project. She is the
author of *Out to Work: A History of Wage-Earning Women in the
United States*, which won the Philip Taft Prize for 1982, and of
other books.

The College of Arts and Sciences is pleased to share the ideas
of a noted historian through our Blazer Lecture Series monograph. Our pleasure is increased by the knowledge that we
have the support of three generations of a distinguished Kentucky family, the Blazers, who recognize the importance of
intellectual pursuits as we explore our culture and our society.

Michael A. Baer, Dean
College of Arts and Sciences
University of Kentucky

Acknowledgments

This book originated as the University of Kentucky Blazer Lectures in April 1988. I am grateful to Nancy Schrom Dye and her colleagues in the History Department and at the university for inviting me to do the lectures, and for their generous hospitality during my stay in Lexington. I also want to thank the Berkshire Conference of Women Historians for asking me to keynote the 1987 conference: an invitation that led me, generally, to start thinking about history in the ways represented here, and, more specifically, to produce the essay that appears at the end of this volume.

As every academic knows, time for research and writing is a blessed commodity. I am very grateful to have received more than my share. During the early stages of research on this project, I benefited from a National Endowment for the Humanities fellowship, supplemented by research grants from Hofstra University. In the final months of its completion, I have been generously supported by the Rockefeller Foundation Gender Roles Program, sadly now defunct. In addition, Temple University enhanced my capacity to complete the project by providing research assistance and other support. The Center for Studies of Social Change, directed by Charles Tilly at the New School for Social Research, has been kind enough to house and inspire me while I experienced the agonies of revision.

Some of the ideas that follow were presented at lectures and seminars at Miami University of Ohio, San Francisco State University, the South West Labor History Association, the Center for Studies of Social Change at the New School for Social

Research, and the University of Maine. Chapter 2 was originally presented at the Conference on Women in the Progressive Period, sponsored by the Smithsonian Institution and the American Historical Association. I want to thank everybody who so generously criticized and commented. Special thanks go to the friends and colleagues who have influenced the development of this manuscript at various stages. Nancy Schrom Dye, Noralee Frankel, Nancy Hewitt, Amy Swerdlow, Carole Turbin, and Marilyn Blatt Young all read portions of it. Linda Kerber and Blanche Wiesen Cook read the entire manuscript, and I am particularly indebted to them for the twin blessings of constructive criticism and enthusiastic encouragement that sparked its completion.

To Jerry Hess, who has now retired from the National Archives, I want to say that a generation of researchers will miss him. He has helped me ferret out sources without which this book could not have taken shape. Katherine Ott and Lisa McGirr provided the best research assistance possible.

I wish I could say how much it has meant to me to share the intellectual companionship, wise counsel, and extraordinary insight of Bert Silverman. His imprint appears on every page of this book. Let me say only that a dedication is not enough by half.

Introduction

I get paid for what I do here, as far as home it can go, I don't care. I don't get paid to work there.
                    —Cotton mill worker to her foreman[1]

If you don't bring home a paycheck there's no gauge for whether you're a success or not a success. People pay you to work because you're doing something useful and you're good at it. But nobody pays a housewife because what difference does it make.
                    —34-year-old typist[2]

A "woman's wage" is a phrase with particular resonance in the modern period. As women struggle to achieve equality in the labor market, the wages that measure their progress creep frustratingly slowly toward the goal of parity with those of men. At the same time, traditional labor market ideology suggests that wage differentials reflect the choices of individuals. It is not that women choose to be paid less, the argument goes, but that they choose lives that yield less certain rewards in the workplace.

Contemporary feminist scholarship illuminates these arguments by challenging the structures on which they rest. Skeptical of received categories of knowledge, it opens to examination a range of issues that might otherwise remain obscured. In the case of women's aspirations, for example, it asks about the parameters of choice; the ways in which choice is constructed; and the gendered limits placed on its conception. Feminist scholarship operates from the assumption that the traditional belief systems out of which knowledge is constructed place constraints on thought that have real consequences for the behavior of individuals who live within them. If we are to use our knowledge to move to a new plane, we need to dissect seemingly natural meanings and to explore how they function in the real world. These essays are offered as illustrations of how that might be done around the idea of the wage in twentieth century United States. They seek to explain historical experience by uniting abstract arguments about the nature of meaning with the forceful reality of an idea of the wage that has shaped the lives of millions of American men and women.

Theoretically, the market treats men and women neutrally, judging only the characteristics of their labor. In the world of economists, the wage is rooted in the play of supply and demand. And then, in acquiescence to the knowledge that there are no perfect markets, it is modified. Depending on the school of economists and its location in space and time, an interpreter may see the wage as a product of more or less rigid laws: the press of population; the productivity of industry; the level of social services; the value of the product produced; and the behavior and expectations of workers. These things and more influence economists' conception of the wage.

Popular perceptions of the wage are far richer than the descriptions of economists would imply. In the popular mind, the wage has nearly always had an adjective attached. Ideas of a "just" wage and a "fair" wage have marked the struggles of working people since the end of the middle ages. In the nineteenth and early twentieth centuries, notions of a "family" wage and a "living" wage dominated discussion of the labor market. During the depression of the 1930s, public disapproval attempted to restrict the work of those who earned a "luxury" wage in favor of those who depended on a "necessity" wage.

These popular images alert us to look at the wage for meanings that transcend the economists' models. They suggest that the wages is neither neutral nor natural but rather contains within it clues to how the laws of economists manifest themselves in the real worlds of human relationships, political compromise, and social struggle. They reveal a set of social constructs hidden inside the wage that convey messages about the nature of the world and about fairness and justice within it. And they suggest a set of gendered instructions that speak to men and women and to the relations between them.

Even a quick comparison opens up these messages. A "man's" wage is a badge of honor. It conjures up images of self-sufficiency and strength, of ordered families, and of just rewards for service performed. A "woman's" wage, in contrast, is frequently a term of opprobrium. It belongs to someone who is not male and therefore not deserving. Historically a measure of women's exploitation, it has become a metaphor for women's place. Earned primarily by women without adequate male support, it became a symbol of family degradation, a mark of poverty, a revelation of family secrets, an attack on social order. Earned by single women, it was a comment on personality and sexuality. The woman's wage was thus uniquely the subject of regulation and control, of discomfort and commentary.

It is worth pausing here to look at the stark realities these metaphors reflect. In 1988, twenty-five years after the Equal Pay Act was signed into law, full-time women workers still earned less than 70 cents for every dollar earned by men. And in 1989, twenty-five years after the passage of the most comprehensive Civil Rights Act in modern times, full-time African-American male workers earned about 73 cents for each dollar earned by white men. White women made 11 cents more an hour than African-American women. None of these figures takes account of unemployment and underemployment, both endemic among all women and people of color. Even so, they tell us that neither Black men nor women of any group earn what is popularly conceived of as a man's wage. Because exclusion from this mark of respect has far more than economic consequences, an attempt to dissect the wage speaks to the most pressing contemporary issue.

If we allow ourselves the leisure to explore the wage as a gendered concept, we discover that the conceptions of male and female contained within it change over time. Because the wage participates in social custom and practice, it embodies the lived realities of male and female sex roles, producing an abiding tension between a market that is said to distinguish only between workers' skills, education, and commitment on the one hand and a set of social constructs that values sexual

difference in various ways on the other. The ongoing negotiation between these two spheres provides a way of seeing both
how gender is inscribed into the wage and how the wage helps
to construct gendered expectations for both men and women.

In its tangible form, as a paycheck or a wage packet, the
wage tells us something about the nature of the labor market,
the opportunities it offers and those it closes off. It speaks to
the choices and aspirations of workers. As it is conceived and
represented by interested third parties such as employers,
policy makers, publicists, social scientists, and government
investigators, the wage conveys a message of social and job-
related expectations, appropriate roles, and social needs. It
reflects the realities of the marketplace and demarcates the
differences—real, imagined, resisted, and desired—between
the sexes. To the individual who earns it, the wage is simultaneously an object of struggle and a source of personal satisfaction and achievement. It is a public statement about the self
and tangible evidence of social value and approval bestowed
on each of us by the world.

These essays attempt to explore some of the complex meanings of the wage as they play themselves out in the twentieth
century United States. Because the wage mediates between
self and society, it represents a crucial set of social relations. It
speaks not merely to the choices that are possible in the world
but to the way choices are conceived and perpetuated. I intend
these essays, then, to illustrate a way of thinking about the past
that illuminates differences within apparently fixed categories. Thus, if the wage is a particularly good way of looking at
the construction of gender within our society, it might be no
less useful for looking at race, or ethnicity, or the values attached to different forms of sexuality. And if ideas about wages
have helped to change the circumstances of male and female
lives, then other such concepts (as for example 'family' or
'welfare') may well have served the same function. I hope that
in demonstrating the complexity of popular conceptions of the
wage, these essays will point the way towards a clearer understanding of how power is exercised and how it resists female
equality.

I have not tried here to achieve the comprehensive approach or the definitive statement of the fully formed journal article. Rather, these essays are intended to be provocative illustrations. Read in chronological order, they trace women's progress from economic dependence to relative independence in the twentieth century and from family to individual lives. They move through the major wage strategies of this century: from family wage, to living wage, to minimum wage, to equal pay, and comparable worth. Read separately, each illustrates the value of a particular stance for illuminating characteristics of the idealized and real wage. The first views the wage from the perspective of policymakers; the second from that of the legal framework; the third takes the position of the wage earner; the fourth locates the wage in political struggle; and the fifth ruminates about some of the theoretical issues in historical perspective. Though each is rooted in a body of empirical data, they are offered in the speculative and reflective spirit of an ongoing conversation. If they cast some light on issues that are at the center of feminist dialogue and, in consequence, open that dialogue to a wider audience, they will have fulfilled their purpose.

1. The Wage Conceived
Value and Need as Measures of a Woman's Worth

> When a person complains that a certain wage rate is
> unduly low, he may be making that judgment in the
> light of what he thinks is due the kind of *person*
> performing that work, e.g. a married man. Others may
> regard the same rate as not unreasonable in view of the
> kind of *work* it is.
>
> —Henry A. Landsberger[1]

In 1915 New York State's Factory Investigating Commission
asked some seventy-five prominent individuals—economists,
social reformers, businessmen, and publicists among them—
what factors determined the rate of wages. The answers varied.
Some suggested that workers' organizations were most important; others believed the size of a business's profits could
enhance or restrain the wages of employees. Another key factor
was the standard of living anticipated by workers. But the
majority of those interviewed believed the efficiency of the
worker and the supply of labor constituted by far the two most
powerful determinants of wages.[2] These traditional explana-
tions for wage rates would have found favor with the proponents of the economic theory then popular.

Widely accepted wage theory at the turn of the century was
rooted in, though not limited to, the law of supply and demand. If that phrase, as economic historian Arnold Tolles
implies, does not do economists justice, it does, at least, convey
the economists' belief "that the reward for every kind of human
effort is controlled by some kind of impersonal and irresistible
force, similar to the force of gravity."[3] Theory held that wages

would rise or fall in response to employers' fluctuating willingness to pay. That willingness in turn was predicated on what employers thought they could earn from labor as well as on how much labor was available at different wage rates. Thus, in theory, the demand for labor (measured by the additional revenue labor could produce) and the supply (which took into account the differences in education and training of the worker) together determined the wage.[4]

Despite the apparent certainty of economists such as Professor Roy Blakely of Cornell who testified before the commission that "wages tend to approximate the value of what they produce,"[5] the theory left room for a substantial degree of subjective judgment on the part of employers as to the value of particular workers. A critical part of the chemical mix that determined the wages of workers in general involved something intangible called "custom." If a male worker was paid according to some formula that reflected the value of what he produced and the difficulty of replacing him, he was also paid according to what he and other workers thought he was worth. Custom, or tradition, played an acknowledged but uncalculated role in regulating the wage. But custom and tradition were gendered. They influenced male and female wages in different ways. And especially in the female wage, they played a far larger role than we have earlier been willing to concede. The women's wage, at least for the early twentieth century, rested in large measure on conceptions of what women needed.

The distinction alerts us to the rich possibilities contained in the wage conceived as a social rather than as a theoretical construct. If the wage is, as most economists readily acknowledge, simultaneously a set of ideas about how people can and should live and a marker of social status, then it contains within it a set of social messages and a system of meanings that influence the way women and men behave. We are all familiar with the capacity of these social meanings to reduce the wages of recent immigrants, of African-Americans, and of other groups. But, partly because it is so apparently natural, the capacity of the wage to speak to issues of gender is less clear.

Yet the language with which the women's wage is conceived throws into relief the same process that exists for men. The wage frames gendered messages; it encourages or inhibits certain forms of behavior; it can reveal a system of meaning that shapes the expectations of men and women and anticipates their struggles over power; it participates in the negotiations that influence the relationships of the sexes inside and outside the family. In all these capacities, the wage functions as a terrain of contest over visions of fairness and justice. This essay will attempt to illustrate some of these processes in the early twentieth century.

The structure of wages that emerged in the course of industrialization in the late nineteenth century reflected a long tradition that revolved around what has become known as the family wage—the sum necessary to sustain family members. That sum had been earned by several family members for most of the history of capitalism. Family income was typically pooled and then redistributed by one family member. But the dream of a family wage that could be earned by a male bread winner alone had long been an object of struggle among organized working people who thought of it as a mechanism for regulating family life and allowing women to work in their own homes.[6] Ideally, and sometimes in practice, the family wage was a male wage, a wage that went to a male breadwinner.[7]

What then of a woman's wage? It reflected not what was but what ought to be. That men ought to be able to support wives and daughters implied that women need not engage in such support. They ought to be performing home duties. Thus, if a woman earned wages, the normal expectation was that she did so to supplement those of other family wage earners. Theoretically, at least, the decision as to who would and would not earn was regulated by the family unit. The wage belonged to her family. Until the third quarter of the nineteenth century, U.S. law and practice reflected these assumptions. Typically, a woman's wage was legally the property of her husband or father. The average wage of women workers was little more than half of the male wage. And even the most skilled women rarely earned as much as two-thirds of the average paid to unskilled men. If a woman lived independently, her wage was normally not sufficient to support her. Nor was it intended to do so.

The nineteenth century fight for a family wage was thus simultaneously a fight for a social order in which men could support their families and receive the services of women; and women, dependent on men, could stay out of the labor force. Historians have debated the advantages and disadvantages of this mode of thinking, but for our purposes it is important to note only that the family wage reflected popular thinking—a sense of what was right and just.[8] Widely supported by working class men and women at the end of the nineteenth century, it rested on what seemed to many to be a desirable view of social order.

Its incarnation in the form of the living wage more clearly isolated the female role. Though the content of a living wage varied, like the family wage, it was imbued with gendered expectations. John Ryan, the Catholic priest who was the United States' most prolific exponent of the living wage, for example, asserted the laborer's right to a "decent and reasonable" life that meant to him "the right to exercise one's primary faculties, supply one's essential needs, and develop one's personality."[9] Others were somewhat more specific. British economist William Smart thought the living wage ought to pay for "a well-drained dwelling, with several rooms, warm clothing with some changes of underclothing, pure water, a plentiful supply of cereal food with a moderate allowance of meat and milk and a little tea, etc., some education, and some recreation, and lastly sufficient freedom for his wife from other work to enable her to perform properly her maternal and her household duties."[10] John Mitchell, head of the United Mine Workers union, was somewhat more ambitious. The wage, he thought, ought to be enough to purchase "the American standard of living." This included, but was not limited to, "a comfortable house of at least six rooms," which contained a bathroom, good sanitary plumbing, parlor, dining room, kitchen, sleeping rooms, carpets, pictures, books, and furniture.[11]

For Ryan, as for other proponents of the living wage, the "love and companionship of a person of the opposite sex"[12] was an essential element of what a living wage should purchase. The bottom line, according to Ryan, was the laborer's capacity "to live in a manner consistent with the dignity of a human being."[13] The *Shoe Workers' Journal* proposed that "everything necessary to the life of *a normal man* be included in the living wage: the right to marriage, the right to have children and to educate them."[14]

As the family wage held the promise of female homemaking, the living wage, which explicitly incorporated wife and children, excluded the possibility that female dignity could inhere either in a woman's ability to earn wages or in her capacity to support a family. Because the living wage idealized a world in which men had the privilege of caring for women and children, it implicitly refused women that privilege. And, because it assumed female dependency, to imagine female independence impugned male roles and male egos. Ground rules for female wage earners required only self-support, and even that was estimated at the most minimal level. Champions of the living wage for women counted among her necessities food, clothing, rent, health, savings, and a small miscellaneous fund.[15] Nothing in the arguments for a female living wage vitiates the harsh dictum of John Stuart Mill. The wages of single women, asserted that famous economist, "must be equal to their support, but need not be more than equal to it; the minimum in their case is the pittance absolutely required for the sustenance of one human being."[16] "Women who are forced to provide their own sustenance have a right," echoed Ryan, "to what is a living wage *for them*." Their compensation, he argued, with apparent generosity, "should be sufficient to enable them to live decently."[17]

At the time Ryan wrote, women constituted close to 25 percent of the industrial work force. More than one-third of wage-earning women in urban areas lived independently of their families, and three-quarters of those living at home helped to support other family members. False conceptions of women who needed only to support themselves did a particular disservice to Black women, who were eight times as likely to earn wages as white women. For Black women racial discrimination and its attendant poverty meant that more that one-third of those who were married would continue to earn wages, and virtually all of those who earned wages participated in family support.[18] Yet the real needs of these women were rarely acknowledged. Nor did the brief, dismissive commentary on "a woman's living wage" mention recreation or comfort or human dignity or the capacity to care for others.

Ryan readily conceded that men without families to support and/or with other means of support were entitled to draw a living wage because "they perform as much labor as their less fortunate fellows."[19] His proposals generously allocated a living wage to men who never intended to marry because "rights are to be interpreted according to the average conditions of human life."[20] But the same generosity was not evident in notions of the living wage for women workers. Rather, it seemed fair to reduce women to the lowest levels of bestiality. Advocates of the living wage confidently explained that women's "standard of physical comfort, in other words, their standard of life" was lower than that of men." While her ideals were "naturally higher than those of men, "her physical wants are simpler. The living wage for a woman is lower than the living wage for a man because it is possible for her as a result of her traditional drudgery and forced tolerance of pain and suffering to keep alive upon less."[21] Women, with a single set of exceptions, were to be paid only according to their most minimal needs. Only to women who were employed in the same jobs as men did Ryan concede the need for equal pay because, he argued, "when women receive less pay than men, the latter are gradually driven out of the occupation."[22]

Ryan failed to acknowledge that in attributing to women "average conditions" that reflected social myth rather than reality he undermined his own cause. While his vision and that of most living wage advocates came from a desire to protect the home, not from antagonism to the pitiable condition of those women who worked for wages, his proposals left the home vulnerable. "The welfare of the whole family," he noted, "and that of society likewise, renders it imperative that the wife and mother should not engage in any labor except that of the household. When she works for hire, she can neither care properly for her own health, rear her children aright, nor make her home what it should be for her husband, her children, herself."[23] Theoretically, that might have been true; but in practice, by reducing women's potential capacity to earn adequate incomes, he diminished their ability to support themselves and their homes.

Without negating the good intentions of Ryan and others on behalf of the family and without imposing anachronistic judgments about their desire to protect the family and to place family needs ahead of women's individual rights, one can still see that the consequences of their rhetoric for women who earned wages were no mere abstractions. They assumed a hard and concrete reality, for example, in discussions of the minimum wage for women that took place between about 1911 and 1913. To alleviate the plight of women workers, social reformers attempted to pass legislation that would force employers to pay a wage sufficient to meet a woman's minimal needs. Between 1912 and 1923, thirteen states and the District of Columbia passed such legislation in one form or another. Each statute was preceded by a preamble that declared the legislators' intentions to offer protection that ranged from providing a sum "adequate for maintenance" to ensuring enough to "maintain the worker in health" and guaranteeing her "moral well-being." Whatever the language of the preamble, and whatever the mechanism by which the wage was ultimately to be decided, the minimum was invariably rooted in what was determined to be a "living" wage for women workers.[24] But the discussion required some estimate of what a living wage might be. Elizabeth Beardsley Butler who surveyed working women in Pittsburgh in 1907 suggested that a woman could "not live decently and be self supporting" at a wage of less than $7 a week. Three years later Louise Bosworth estimated the living wage of Boston's women ranged from $9 to $11 a week—the first amount would keep a woman from dying of cold or hunger; the second provided the possibility of efficiency at work and some minimal recreation.[25] The question, said social pundit Thomas Russell, was whether "it is to be an amount that shall provide only the bare necessaries of life or shall it include some provision for comforts, recreation and the future?"[26]

The budgets drawn up by experts generally opted only for the necessities. Arrived at after extensive surveys to uncover the actual expenditures of "working girls," and heavily reliant on language and imagery that reduced women to perpetual girlhood, they included almost nothing beyond the barest sustenance.[27] A typical survey was undertaken by Sue Ainslee Clark in 1908 and published by Clark and Edith Wyatt in the pages of *McClure's* magazine in 1910.[28] The authors focused on the effortful struggle to make ends meet, turning survival itself into a praiseworthy feat. They exuded sympathy for the girl who "ate no breakfast," whose "luncheon consisted of coffee and rolls for ten cents," and who, as "she had no convenient place for doing her own laundry, . . . paid 21 cents a week to have it done. Her regular weekly expenditure was as follows: lodging, 42 cents; board, $1.40; washing, 21 cents; clothing and all other expenses, $1.97: total, $4."[29] Such estimates encouraged social investigators to define precisely how much a female wage earner might spend for everything from undergarments to gifts.

The debate over the minimum wage revealed what this outward order dictated: to live alone required the strictest exercise of thrift, self-discipline, and restraint. The budgets warned fiercely against expectations of joy, spontaneity, pleasure, or recreation. Even the carfare that might provide access to a walk in the country was rigidly restricted. The wage prescribed a spartan life-style, sufficient, it was hoped, to preserve morality for those destined to earn but not so generous as to tempt those in families to live outside them. It limited fantasy to the price of survival and held open the door of ambition only to a meagre independence. Its effects are grimly reflected in a series of snippets selected by and published in *Harper's Bazar* in 1908 under the title "The Girl Who Come To the City."[30]

Offering to pay $5 for each one it used, the magazine solicited brief essays "written by those girl readers who have gone

through the experience of coming to the city, and either suc-
ceeding or failing there during the last ten years."[31] Success, in
these pieces, is measured in small and treasured doses. Mere
survival emerges as a potent source of satisfaction. In a period
when most experts estimated a living wage at around $9 a
week, a pay envelope that amounted to $10 a week could yield
happiness. A $2 a week raise, accompanied by a kind boss, and
perhaps the chance to improve oneself by reading occasionally
at work seemed to be the height of ambition.[32] At the top of the
wage scale, a bookkeeper could aspire to $65 a month, enough
to ensure a small cash balance in the bank if one limited social
excursions to one night a week and carefully selected clothes
from among sale items.[33] The stories reveal justified pride and
accomplishment in the ability to sustain oneself. But they also
tell us something of the limits imposed on women's aspirations. "I had," boasted one contributor about the period before
she returned home, "made both ends meet financially for five
months and I had saved a modest sum for the purchase of a
winter suit."[34] Even women who needed help in the form of
occasional contributions of clothing felt they had managed
very nicely.

And yet, in practice, survival was the best, not the worst,
that the wage embodied. The estimates made by well-inten-
tioned reformers and the efforts of the most well-meaning
women were compromised by the refusal of most employers to
concede a woman's need even to support herself. Evidence for
this is part of the folklore of the female labor market before
World War II and has frequently been recorded by historians.[35] The *Harper's Bazar* series is no exception. There, as
elsewhere, women recalled how difficult it was to ask for
reasonable compensation. A stenographer described how a
lawyer had refused to pay more because "he expected young
women had friends who helped them out." A budding news
reporter was told by a potential employer that his "rule is
never to employ a woman who must depend entirely upon my
salaries."[36]

The aspirations of young women thus fell victim to the self-
confirming myths that enforced their dependence. Nineteenth

century British economist William Smart described the process succinctly. Part of the reason a woman's wage is low, he suggested, was "because she does not require a high wage, whether it be because her father partly supports her, or because her maintenance does not cost so much."[37] Employers routinely acted upon this myth. "We try to employ girls who are members of families," a box manufacturer told social investigator and economist Elizabeth Butler, "for we don't pay the girls a living wage in this trade."[38] Historian Joanne Meyerowitz summed up the prevailing attitude this way: "Employers assumed that all working women lived in families where working males provided them with partial support. It profited employers to use this idealized version of the family economy to determine women's wages."[39]

For all the elaborate theory justifying low wages, the bottom line turned out almost always to be the employer's sense of what was acceptable. Men, as Elizabeth Butler noted, came into occupations at a wage paid for the job. Women came into them at a wage deemed appropriate for female workers—not, that is to say, at the customary wage level of the occupation but "at a level analogous to that paid women generally in other occupations."[40] New York City social worker Mary Alden Hopkins told the Factory Investigating Commission that the sex of the employee was one of the most important influences on women's wages. "In laundry work, factory work, some mercantile establishments and home work, efficiency has little and often no effect upon wages," she declared.[41] The hardest woman's job, in her judgment, was the lowest paid, and an increase in worker productivity and employer profits led less often to rewarding workers than to discharging high-paid workers in favor of those who could be paid for less. The young Scott Nearing summarized the process this way: "No one even pretends that there is a definite relation between the values produced by the workers and the wage which he secures."[42] Samuel Gompers would have agreed: "Everyone knows that there is little connection between the value of services and wages paid; the employer pays no more than he must."[43]

While from the economist's perspective this may be a gross

oversimplification, employers, workers, and observers all accepted the critical importance of custom in the wage structure. A vice-president of the Pullman Company, speaking before the commission that investigated the great strike of 1894, acknowledged as much. Piece rates, he said, were based on the company's estimates of a "reasonable wage for ten hours . . . for a competent workman." If the company discovered "that at the piece price fixed the known less competent and less industrious workmen are regularly making an unreasonable day's wage, it becomes apparent that the piece price allotted is too large."[44] At issue here was what was "reasonable" and "unreasonable," not the productivity or efficiency of the worker. In this context, that part of the content of custom should rest on the sex of the worker appears to be merely natural. An official of International Harvester, testifying before an Illinois investigating commission in 1912, described his company's efforts to set a minimum wage for female employees. His company's desire, he claimed, "was to establish a minimum that would be fair and reasonable." But the constraints of what was deemed reasonable were established as much by the nature and characteristics of the worker as by the company's financial spread sheets. "The girls affected by lower wages," he said in mitigation, "are mostly of foreign birth. They are not required to dress up for their employment. Many of those to whom we will pay $8 could not earn a dollar downtown."[45] Presumably, the same kind of reasoning led to paying Black women less than white women. Although occupational segregation accounts for most of the wage differential between Black and white women, Black women who worked on the same kinds of jobs routinely received one dollar a week less.

Nor was the weight of custom in setting wages a hidden dimension. Rather, the comments of employers and others reveal it to have been quite conscious and available. Several respondents to the Factory Investigating Commission's survey noted its influence in setting wage rates, pointing out that wages could not be set without reference to such factors as the "needs of the individual and family," the influence of "local or trade union conditions," and the differential requirements of "pin-money workers." Edward Page, an officer of the Merchants' Association of New York, thought that the "customary or habitual rate of wages which prevails in the group to which the workingman belongs and which is usual in the industry under consideration . . . is by far the most important factor in the determination of wages."[46] On their face these factors were gender neutral. But since each embodied deeply rooted aspects of gendered expectations, the wage both reflected and perpetuated gendered behavior.

If the role of custom in fixing wages is not surprising, and we can take for granted that sex played a part, then we need ask only to what degree the sex of the worker influenced custom. When it came to women, one might argue that custom played not the smallest but the largest part in determining the wage. William Smart placed the factors that determined the wages of women in the category of "wants." The wage scale in a modern industrial economy, he suggested, was typically determined by "what a worker does." But for a woman "what the worker is" was the gauge of wages. The difference made him uneasy. "If a male worker," he asked, "is supposed to get a high wage when he produces much, a low wage when he produces little, why should a woman's wage be determined by another principle? We cannot hunt with the individualist hounds and run with the socialist hare."[47]

Yet women's wages at the turn of the century clung stubbornly to what Smart would have called her "wants" rather than to either the value of the product or the level of the worker's productivity. For if custom was inscribed into the wage and the wage was conceived male, what women earned was not in the same sense as males a "wage." In the minds of employers and of male workers, the wage was to be paid to those who supported families.[48] If part of its function was to reflect the value of the product made, another and equally important part was to make a statement about the value of the worker who made the product. As long as female workers were not—could not be—male workers, their wages could not hope to touch those of their male peers.

We can guess that employers thought of it that way by their

responses to questions about how much they paid women. Louise Bosworth cited the case of a woman who told her employer, "We cannot live on what we earn," and was asked in response, "Then what wages can you live on?"[49] The same paternalistic assumptions appear among employers who testified before the commission that investigated Illinois's white slave traffic in 1912. The employers interviewed reported unhesitatingly that they paid their male and female workers on the basis of what they estimated each needed. Julius Rosenwald, head of Sears, Roebuck and Company, then a mail-order house, told an investigative commission that "the concern made it a point not to hire girls not living at home at less than $8 a week."[50] A Montgomery Ward vice-president echoed the sentiment: "We claim that all our employees without homes are on a self-supporting basis, and if we discover they are not we will put them there in an hour."[51] One department store executive described how his store asked all job applicants to sign a form "giving their estimate of necessary expenses in addition to family particulars. The girls who are not receiving sufficient to live on come to us. There are many instances of such receiving an increase." No one ever investigated the accuracy of the application forms, and even the commission chair was dubious as to who the procedure protected. A girl might readily lie about home support, he noted, "to assure herself of a job."[52] But at bottom, this was less the issue than the prevailing assumption that "girls" could and should be paid at a minimum that relied on family subsidy rather than on what their labor was worth.

If employers and popular opinion are any guide, and the question of what appeared to be reasonable lay at the heart of the wage structure, then all wages—not only those of women—contained a greater proportion of wants than most of us have recognized. Women's wages, then, are only uniquely vulnerable in the sense that they participate in popular definitions of gender that denigrate the needs of one sex. The wage simultaneously framed job-related expectation in the light of existing gender roles and shaped gender experiences to avoid disappointment in view of the prevailing wage structure. More than exploitation of women, or paternalism towards them, the wage reflected a rather severe set of injunctions about how men and women were to live. These injunctions could be widely negated only at the peril of social order. Thus, part of the function of the female wage was to ensure attachment to family. The male wage, in contrast, provided incentives to individual achievement. It promoted geographical mobility and sometimes hinted at the possibility of social mobility as well. The female wage allowed women to survive; the male wage suggested a contribution to national economic well-being. These messages affirmed existing values and integrated all the parties into a set of understandings that located the relationships of working men and women to each other.

Some of these messages are powerful. Existing wage fund theory posited a limited sum available for all wages. It reduced the incentive to provide a higher wage for women by suggesting that their gain would come at the cost of male raises and therefore threaten the family's well-being. Smart put it this way: "Women's wages are, after all, part and parcel of the one share in the distribution of income which falls to labor."[53] What followed from that, of course, was that raising women's wages would merely reduce those of the men in their class by a similar proportion, leaving families in the same place economically and depriving them of maternal care to boot. Samuel Gompers translated this into a warning to members of the American Federation of Labor: "In industries where the wives and children toil, the man is often idle because he has been supplanted, or because the aggregate wages of the family are no higher than the wages of the adult man—the husband and father of the family."[54]

If women's wage gains could come only at the cost of the family, then their low wages affirmed and supported existing family life. As the renowned economist Alfred Marshall put it, a higher wage for women might be "a great gain in so far as it tends to develop their faculties, but an injury in so far as it tempts them to neglect their duty of building up a true home, and of investing their efforts in the personal capital of their children's character and abilities."[55] To Marshall the clear social choice implicit in the wage payment was between individual achievement and family well-being. His statement affirms the use of wages to preserve what is desirable to him: that all women are or will be married, that marriage is a normal state, that women will be continuously supported by men with sufficient wages, and that under these circumstances a wage that might be translated into an incentive not to marry or remain within families poses a challenge. Moreover, Marshall's view reflected the prevailing belief that a man was entitled to a wife to serve him and their home. It contained the assumption that a female who did not have a husband had erred. The differential female wage thus carried a moral injunction, a warning to women to follow the natural order.

The absence, by choice or necessity, of a family of her own did not excuse a woman from adherence to familial duties or morals, nor did it impel a more generous attitude toward wages. In fact, the level of the wage, which signaled an affirmation of family life, simultaneously threw out a challenge to preserve morality. In a March 1913 letter to the *New York Herald*, the head of Illinois's vice commission commented that "out investigations . . . show conclusively that thousands of good girls are going wrong every year merely because they can not live upon the wages paid them by employers."[56] But this was not necessarily an invitation to raise wages. Since not to live within a family was itself immoral, and the wage was seen as primarily a contribution to family life, a higher wage would only contribute to immorality. An ongoing debate over the fine line between a wage high enough to tempt women into supporting themselves and one so low that it could push the unwary into prostitution placed the wage in thrall to morality. Social worker Jeannette Gilder found herself in the awkward position of testifying against a pay raise for working women because "it seems to me to be paying a pretty poor compliment to the young women of this country to suggest that their virtue hangs upon such a slender thread that its price can be fixed somewhere between $6 and $8 a week."[57] And yet those who insisted that a low wage was an invitation to prostitution dominated the debate.

The wage also transmitted messages about the work force. Employers feared that a rise in women's wages would trigger a demand for higher wages for men. As the wage captured social restrictions on female aspirations at work, so it conveyed the male potential for advancement, promotion, loyalty, and persistence. Contemporaries understood this well. When Elizabeth Butler remarked that "boys are often preferred to girls . . . because they can be relied on to learn the trade and women cannot,"[58] she captured the notion that implicit in the wage is the assumption that a man's wage is an investment in the future, while a woman's wage assumes only that the work at hand will be done. Economist Francis Walker said this in a different way. If a man marries, he "becomes a better and more notable workman on that account." In contrast, if a woman marries, "it is most probable that she will . . . be a less desirable laborer than she was before."[59] Yet these statements promote the self-fulfilling function they simultaneously reflect. Lacking a man's wage, women were not normally given the opportunity to demonstrate that they too could be an investment in the future. Such experiments would be dangerous. Not only would a higher wage for women convey an inaccurate estimate of the potential occupational mobility of females, but it might inhibit the employer's capacity to use wages to construct the work force to his liking.

Finally, the wage made a familiar statement about female personality. Holding the stereotypical male as the norm, it claimed recompense for the costs of translating female qualities into the marketplace. Francis Walker exaggerated but caught the point when he insisted that the wage reflected women's character traits as well as their domestic orientation. It took account, he noted, of personalities that were "intensely sensitive to opinion, [and] shrink from the familiar utterances of blame." Coldness and indifference alone, he thought, were often sufficient to repress women's "impulses to activity."[60] These qualities of character exacted supervisory costs of the employer that were recaptured in the lower pay of women. As Charles Cheney, a South Manchester, Connecticut, manufacturer, put it, part of the reason women were paid less than men was because "they are sensitive and require extraordinarily tactful and kindly treatment and much personal consideration."[61]

Restrictive as the messages thrown out by a woman's wage were clearly intended to be, they were by no means the only messages that reached women. The very existence of a wage, the possibility of earning income evoked a contrary set of images: images that derived some support from the promise of American success. The same wage that evoked a struggle to survive and placed a lid on social mobility, the same wage that obscured women's visions of independence and citizenship had the capacity to conjure contrary images as well. It could even point the way to potential equality for women. These tensions are visible in the huge strikes that wracked the garment industry beginning in 1909-10, in the energy of young female labor leaders, and in the quest of more affluent women for lives that combined career and motherhood. Such events indicate that the notion of wages rooted in wants existed in a contested sphere—tempered by a broader ideology of individualism. They lead us to wonder about the role played by a woman's wage in a period of changing wants and rising levels of personal ambition.

The wage that in some measure helped to affirm and construct gendered expectations in the period before World War I continued to play that role afterward. But the dramatic social changes that came during and after the war, particularly the rise of a consumer culture, created their own pressures on the structure of gender. Because for most people the wage offered access to consumption, it mediated some of the tensions in gender roles that emerged in the 1920s. While public perception of a woman's wage remained conceptually "needs-based," continuing to limit female expectations, it quickly became clear that changing needs demanded some concessions to women's individual aspirations. These mixed messages contributed to arguments among women about who deserved a wage.[62]

In the statistical tables, the war appears as a small blip in the history of working women. New entrants into the labor force were relatively few, and the teens ended with little apparent increase in the numbers of women who earned wages. But the big surprise lay in the numbers of women who switched jobs. About half a million women, it seemed, chose to move into men's jobs. The *New York Times* commented on these figures with surprise: "The world of men woke up and took a second look at the world of women during the World War. It is still looking." And, it continued, "the Great War has in many cases been responsible for a change of premise as well as job."[63]

The primary explanation for these job shifts seems to have been the attraction of the male wage. Historian Maurine Greenwald estimates, for example, that women who became streetcar conductors immediately increased their wages by about one-third over those they had earned in traditional female jobs.[64] Daniel Nelson, who has explored the transformation of the factory, notes that after 1915 "the wages offered by machinery and munitions makers" drew an increasing number of women who had worked in traditional women's fields.[65] Though women's productivity was frequently acknowledged to be as high as that of the men they replaced, women were not, on principle, offered the same wage. A twenty-six city survey by the New York State Industrial Commission at the end of the war revealed that less than 10 percent of the women who replaced men received pay equal to that of the men who had preceded them. The commission reported that "in many cases the production of women was equal to that of men, in others it was greater, and in still others, less. The wages paid had little, if anything, to do with productive efficiency."[66] Since women who were paid less than men still earned far more than they could have at women's jobs, few of those who benefited from wartime opportunities complained. But the pressure of a dual wage structure on male wages posed a problem. Fearing a breakdown of social order, men and women began to call for a wage paid for the job—or equal pay. This slogan, as we will see later, was designed primarily to reduce pressure on men's wages.

Though most of the wartime job shifts proved to be temporary, they signaled an incipient dissatisfaction among some wage-earning women over the issue of wages—a dissatisfaction that could no longer be contained by rationalizations over social role. These struggles frequently pitted women who earned wages against those who did not, revealing something about contested definitions of womanhood among white women. For example, when female streetcar conductors in several large cities waged largely futile battles to hang on to their high-paying jobs, they were fighting not only the men who wanted their jobs back but a conception of womanliness that restricted access to outdoor work. And the female printers in New York State who successfully struggled to exempt themselves from legislation that precluded their working during the lucrative night hours simultaneously attacked rigid conceptions of family life.

Such campaigns were opposed by clear signals from government and corporations to women not to expect too much. The Women's Bureau of the Department of Labor offers a case in point. In 1920, when the bureau was created, it received a meagre $75,000 lump-sum appropriation and distributed it as effectively as it could. In 1922 a House proviso "stipulated that no salary in the Women's Bureau should be more than $1800, except three at $2000, and the director's and assistant director's salaries which have been fixed by statute." If effected, the proviso, as the Women's Bureau pointed out, would have left it with "no staff of technically trained, experienced people to direct and supervise its work." But more important, the bureau noted that other agencies of the government paid their male employees with the same qualifications "very much higher salaries than any that have even been suggested by the Women's Bureau—twice as much in many instances."[67]

Such policies were routine in industry. In the electrical industry of the 1920s, Ronald Schatz reports that "corporations maintained separate pay scales for men and women.

Male wage keysheets began where female keysheets left off; the least skilled male workers earned more than the most capable female employee."[68] Still, the point for women was that even this low pay exceeded that of such traditionally female jobs as laundry work and waiting on tables. "For this reason, many young women preferred jobs in electrical factories." When the Ford Motor Company instituted a $5 day for its male employees after the war, it deliberately omitted women workers. According to Vice-President James Couzens, women "are not considered such economic factors as men."[69]

Corporations carefully distinguished between the kinds of social welfare programs offered as extensions of cash wages to women and men. General Electric and Westinghouse offered men programs that stressed financial and job security such as a 5 percent bonus every six months after five years of service; a pension after twenty years, and group life insurance and paid vacations after ten years of service. Women, for whom longevity was not encouraged and for whom it was thought not to matter, got programs that emphasized sociability such as "dances, cooking classes, secretarial instruction, picnics, clubs, and summer camps."[70]

The not-so-subtle relationship between policy and practice is beautifully illustrated in the self-confirming apparatus in effect at the General Electric company where President Gerard Swope defended his policies on the grounds that "our theory was that women did not recognize the responsibilities of life and were hoping to get married soon and would leave us, and therefore, this insurance premium deduction from the pay would not appeal to them."[71] As historian Ronald Schatz notes, because GE compelled women to quit if they married, women rarely acquired enough seniority to obtain pensions or vacations with pay. Women's aspirations could not be entirely stilled by these measures. The Ford Motor Company, according to historian Stephen Meyer III, "considered all women, regardless of their family stakes, as youths: that is as single men under twenty-two without dependents, and therefore ineligible for Ford profits." Yet "as the result of criticism from women's rights advocates, the company eventually allowed some women, who were the heads of households, to participate in its welfare plan."[72]

One result of such policies and an instrument in their perpetuation as well was that women carefully rationalized their increasing work force participation and defended themselves by comparing their wages only to those of other women. The model was familiar. The numerous investigating commissions of the prewar period had already asserted the injustice of paying women as much as men. Thus, investigators exploring the feasibility of a higher wage for women raised such issues as what, for instance, a firm would "have to pay a man with a family if it paid $2 a day to girls with no one but themselves to support?"[73] This does not seem to have inhibited women's desire for higher incomes. But it seems to have channeled their grievances away from men who earned far more than they and toward women instead. Among Western Electric workers interviewed in the late 1920s, a typical female who complained about wages tended to be distressed not at her absolute wage but at how it compared with those of other women. As one female employee complained, "the girl next to me, her job pays $39.80 per hundred, and mine pays $28.80 and I work just as hard as she does. I don't see how they figure that out. She makes ten cents more on every one she makes."[74]

These powerful and sometimes explicit barriers extended across race lines and to the social wages offered by modern corporations. In their presence Black women were paid less than white women for the same or similar jobs. Employers utilized them to sanction distinctions in the amenities they offered to Black and white women. An early survey of the tobacco industry in Virginia reflects the value of such circumscribed comparisons. "Tuesday and Friday," the report noted matter of factly, "the white girls have 15 minutes extra in order to dance, but the 15 minutes is paid for by the firm."[75]

What kept the "wage" pot bubbling, then, was not women's desire to achieve male pay but their urge to satisfy more concrete wants. As mass production jobs and clerical work opened up to white women, some factory jobs became available to Black women. New, relatively well-paying jobs and rising real wages for both men and women contributed to the advent of the consumer society and helped to create a new definition of wants that drew on a prevailing individualism from which women could hardly be excluded. Marketing techniques, installment buying, and the increasing value placed on consumption replaced thrift and postponed gratification as appropriate spirits of the time. New definitions of wants attracted new groups of women to the work force and suggested new rationales for staying there.

The changing population of female workers challenged perceptions of a wage that spoke to simpler needs. To women for whom the prewar women's wage had offered little apart from the despair of poverty, the wage now stretched to encompass the hope of individual achievement measured by material goals. Defined in prewar practice as the minimum required to sustain a single woman partially supported by her family, the postwar wage at least suggested the capacity to earn a living.[76] Ronald Edsforth, who studied auto workers in the 1920s, notes that government investigators discovered among the women working in auto factories in the 1920s a "genuinely modern level of individual materialism . . . guiding . . . life-shaping decisions." They concluded that "jobs in the auto factories were most desired simply because auto workers' earnings were high."[77] But even the rising wage was clearly inadequate to reconcile the competing needs of an increasingly heterogeneous group of female wage earners. Less immigrant than native born, containing a small but steadily growing proportion of married women, and with a still tiny but slowly growing representation of Black women in mainstream jobs that had long been closed to them, women with competing views of the wage attempted to participate in what some called the "American standard of living." In the process they helped to establish a new set of gendered definitions about self and others.

For middle class, single, adventurous women, work and a wage meant escape from boredom, a bit of rebellion, a purpose in life—the means to a relatively autonomous existence. Fuelled by the rhetoric of the women's movement and energized by a successful campaign for the vote, single women, no longer subsidized by families and increasingly eager to live outside them, craved the independence that wages potentially offered. To some, participation in wage work offered to contribute economic equality to the political citizenship they had won with suffrage.[78] To others, as economist Theresa Wolfson suggested, the wage bought the liberty to live "comparatively free lives outside of their working hours."[79]

For poorer women, including immigrants and women of color, and for most of the married women who earned, the wage became a measure of the capacity to participate in an increasingly pervasive consumer society. "I would like to work," commented one young assembly line worker, "until I get my furniture paid for. My husband is young and hasn't got much of a start yet and I want to help him."[80] A woman's wage represented, still, a supplement to male earnings—an extension of family life. Less a vehicle to sheer survival in the 1920s, it promised access to the new wants generated by an ethic of consumption. If it still continued to preclude freedom for most women, it offered a way to sustain and even enhance family life and exacted, in return, the price of women's continuing commitment to the work force.[81] It should not surprise us then that the changing material content of the wage did not diminish either the effort to earn it or its importance in women's lives. And it dramatically expanded the numbers of women willing and able to earn wages. A young woman who had worked at the Western Electric company for a year complained that her feet swelled on the job. She didn't want to sit down, however, because "I can't turn out the rates when I sit down." She had, she said, returned to Western Electric after a year at another job because "I couldn't earn near as much money, and I couldn't save any."[82]

Because a woman's wage had to serve the increasingly fragmented needs of a diverse array of women, the rhetoric surrounding it became more complex. It is best uncovered in the efforts of the newly created Women's Bureau of the Department of Labor to represent women workers of all kinds. The bureau's official position consistently upheld wages for women based on the value of the job. Yet its public posture simultaneously affirmed the need for a minimum wage based on the needs of the worker. Wages, wrote Mary Anderson, head of the bureau, "should be established on the basis of occupation and not on the basis of sex or race." At the same time, she added, the minimum wage rate that was available to women only, if at all, "should cover the cost of living in health and decency, instead of a bare existence, and should allow for dependents and not merely for the individual."[83]

The compromise, then, appeared to lie not in abandoning a needs-based assessment of women's wages so much as in an effort to understand that any definition of "wants" encompassed a broad range of human needs. While fewer than 15 percent of all married women, and about 30 percent of Black married women, with wage-earning husbands were regularly employed before the 1930s, those who earned wages had a complicated series of wants. For example, well-paid male and female hosiery workers in the Piedmont Valley of North Carolina and Tennessee flaunted their capacity to buy consumer goods.[84] In the same region, the poorly paid white textile workers could and frequently did hire Black women to take care of their children while white husbands and wives worked in the mills.[85] Black women used their tiny pay to feed and clothe their children and to support those who cared for them in their absence. Such enormous differences in the uses of wages notwithstanding, the image of women paid at a rate regulated by public perceptions of abstract needs helped to perpetuate the sense that, in the competition for jobs among women, what was at stake was not skill or the nature of work but the capacity to contribute to family support. This image perpetuated a low wage for all women. In exactly the way that employers had earlier chosen to believe that young, single women were supported by their parents, so, in the period after World War I, an idealized image of marriage with its attendant financial subsidy served to define a woman's role and threatened to regulate the level of wages for all women.

Partly in consequence, single women, inside and outside the Women's Bureau, were haunted by visions of married women

subsidized by their husbands and therefore able to accept
lower wages. Public debate over the wage question in the 1920s
turned on the issue of whose needs the wage was intended to
meet—the married woman working for "pin money" or the
independent self-supporting woman of all classes. Neither category encompassed the reality of women workers, more than
three-quarters of whom, according to contemporary studies,
supported themselves and their families. While in the prewar
period, questions about "workers who are in part supported by
parents or other members of the family"[86] had captured a
certain unease about independent women who transcended
traditional roles, the 1920s attack on "pin money" workers
focused on the distress of single working women who feared
competition from women whose families partially supported
them. The competition, muted by the prosperity of the 1920s,
did not explode until the 1930s. In the meantime, the question
of married women in industry was argued pro and con, with
such stalwart champions of working women as Mary Gilson,
Melinda Scott, and Sophonisba Breckinridge protesting that
married women ought not to be in the labor force. Breckinridge proposed instead "a living wage for men based on their
own needs and those of their wives and a standard family of
three children; disciplinary measures for husbands who are
unwilling to work, and state aid for wives of those who cannot
work."[87]

In the face of the commitment to a needs-based wage, proponents of individualism and some champions of the Women's
Bureau fought a losing battle for "a rate for the job." The new
consumerism required a more complex set of messages than
simple individualism. While it offered support for raising the
wage enough to accommodate both new social relations and
new needs, it would not, and did not, challenge conceptions of
the wage that sustained family life. Thus, one group of women
struggled to elevate a woman's wage by asking that all workers
receive value for the job, while a second declared itself in need
of protective legislation and advocated a minimum wage to
legitimate women's capacity to work at all. A woman's wage
still refused to incorporate the capacity to earn a living. At

most, it offered a fling at independence to those who did not need to contribute to family support. For the poor it could enhance a family's standard of living. But in no sense was a woman's wage intended to promote the desire for a self-sufficient existence.

Yet to women who worked, the capacity to improve the standard of living was not mere ideology. The reification of an "American" standard of living offered a rationale for continuing wage work among married women. As consumer expectations rose, the purchase of what some might have called pin money goods became not luxuries but part of the quality of life. Because a woman's wage appeared as largely contributory, it neither undermined male egos nor fomented female independence. Men understood the wage as an indication of whether they were "getting ahead." Women understood it as an indication of whether they could keep up with their work, their status among their peers, and their position in the eyes of the boss. And yet women's capacity to enhance the family standard contributed to denuding the notion that the family wage either could or should be earned by men alone. At the same time, women established new sources of comparisons that enabled them to maintain status and self-esteem even as they continued to earn less than two-thirds of the wage of the average male worker.

But women's wages, restricted by an ethos of need and locked into comparisons with other women, still could not rise high enough to compete with the wages of men. If the message of the wage differed for men and women, it failed to prevent women from seeking the same kinds of material gains acquired by men. At some level the "woman's wage" decisively relegated females to a plateau of citizenship that could not be equated with that of men. As much as suffrage had seemed to extend citizenship to women, a woman's wage suggested the limits of their aspirations and assigned them to sometimes objectionable social roles. A "rate for the job"—a wage equivalent to that of similarly situated men working in the same firm—would have trumpeted a message of aspiration and ambition that few in the 1920s were ready to hear. But the value that a woman worker created was never the central issue of women's wage work. Rather, the wage sought to identify the boundaries within which economic inequality could be used to constrain the prerogatives of citizenship. The sex of a worker remained safely more important than what that worker did. With some few exceptions, equality was not at issue; the wage did not contest male prerogatives in the workplace. Rather, it symbolized the limits of political citizenship.

2. Law and a Living

The Gendered Content of "Free Labor" in the Progressive Period

What could possibly be more contemptible than the
question; "What is the least sum on which an honest girl
can keep body and soul together and escape disgrace?"
—Florence Kelley[1]

Supreme Court decisions are frequently unpopular. Yet few
have faced the storm of national derision that confronted the
April 1923 opinion handed down in *Adkins* v. *Children's Hospital*. By a vote of 5 to 3 (Brandeis abstaining), the Court negated
the constitutionality of a Washington, D.C., law that provided
minimum wages for women and minors. With its act the Court
also placed in jeopardy the minimum wage legislation of thirteen other states.[2]

Newspaper editorials, public meetings, and placards denounced the decision. Mary Anderson, head of the Women's
Bureau, called it "nothing short of a calamity."[3] Samuel Gompers declared it to be a "logical next step in perfecting the
doctrine that those who cannot help themselves shall not be
helped."[4] The *New York World* ran a cartoon that depicted
Justice Sutherland handing the document to a woman wage
earner, with the caption, "This decision, madam, affirms your
constitutional right to starve."[5] In the immediate aftermath of
the decision, the National Women's Trade Union League called
a conference to stave off what it feared would be "a wholesale
reduction of wages for more than 1,500,000 women and girls."[6]
The "greatest wrong" in the decision, as Gompers and others

pointed out, was that in describing labor as a commodity to be bought and sold Justice Sutherland had likened "the labor of a woman to the purchase of a shinbone over the counter to make soup."[7] Henry Seager, respected professor of economics at Columbia University, fulminated that the decision "represents a menace to the stability of our established institutions vastly more serious than that of socialists, communists, bolshevists, or any other group of 'labor agitators.'"[8] Many opponents of the decision decried the Court's power to declare laws unconstitutional or urged that it be severely restricted. Henceforth, they suggested, six or seven rather than a bare majority of five justices should be required to repudiate any state law.[9]

The response might have been louder because the decision was apparently so unexpected. Fifteen years earlier, in *Muller* v. *Oregon*, the Court had accepted the principle that women's health was a proper subject of state concern and therefore of state regulation.[10] In the wake of that decision, most industrial states had taken it upon themselves to regulate the hours and working conditions of women and minors. These laws, quintessentially progressive in that they attempted to redress the imbalances of rapid industrial growth, had withstood many legal challenges and, just a year after Adkins, were to survive another. Though states were more cautious when it came to regulating wages, thirteen states and the District of Columbia had enacted minimum wage laws before 1923. Each was grounded in the assumption that the needs of working women for food, clothing, and shelter could be accurately determined and in the desire to maintain women's health and protect their morals by establishing wages at a level "adequate to supply the necessary cost of living."[11]

Minimum wage laws varied. Some set wage levels. Others established regulatory commissions to determine appropriate wages. Some provided legal penalties for violators. Others relied on public exposure to inhibit transgression. They had weathered many challenges in state courts. And, in 1917, the U.S. Supreme Court, in an equally divided vote, affirmed an Oregon Supreme Court decision to uphold its minimum wage law.[12] These successful defenses of minimum wage laws led one commentator to note in 1921 that "no successful attack can be anticipated upon the principle of these laws in view of the absolute uniformity with which they have been maintained in the different states when pressed to a decision in the court of last resort."[13] Moreover, they were popular. Even after Adkins, states like Massachusetts and Washington continued to enforce their statutes, hoping to evade legal challenges; others, like New York, passed new laws.[14] Why then had the Court so unexpectedly countered what seemed like a well-established trend?

The answer may lie in the competing paradigms embedded in the issue of minimum wages for women. Decisions about minimum wages were grounded both in legal precedents around labor and in those around women. Watching the judiciary confront these issues tells us something about the vital importance of the idea of gender differences in the progressive era. And looking at the evolution of the relationship between a doctrine grounded in changing theories of labor and one that rested on separate spheres may tell us something about the relationship of gender differences to other influential ideas in the construction of law and social policy. As we examine the roots of Adkins, we begin to understand something of how the gendered content of ideas governed an important set of political and judicial decisions and, not inadvertently, laid the groundwork for incorporating nineteenth century notions of workers' dignity and independence into the judicial system.

Minimum wage legislation derived its rationale from the gendered arguments used to gain passage of other regulatory legislation.[15] Its purpose, as the title of the Oregon Act makes clear, was "to protect the lives and health and morals of women and minor workers . . . ," or, as the District of Columbia Act put it, "to protect women and minors from conditions detrimental to their health and morals, resulting from wages which are inadequate to maintain decent standards of living."[16] As such, it was firmly rooted in progressive notions of women's separate sphere. Wage-earning women, in the familiar words of *Muller* v. *Oregon*, deserved protection because the "two sexes differ in structure of body, in the functions to be performed by each, in the amount of physical strength, in the capacity for

long-continued labor . . . in the capacity to maintain the struggle for subsistence."[17] The widely accepted notion that women
were mothers of the race provided more than adequate justification for the courts to regulate women's working lives. But
although the courts in earlier decisions had accepted sex difference as a reasonable basis for restraining the freedom of
women and employers to contract, and would subsequently
continue to rely on sex difference, the Supreme Court rejected
the idea in Adkins.

In so doing, the Court simply affirmed what had been well
established by 1923, namely that an individual's freedom to
contract was not subject to restraint by the state, unless the
public welfare was affected. The decision was rooted in nineteenth century arguments over free labor. As Justice Sutherland noted, freedom of contract while not absolute was "the
general rule, and restraint the exception."[18] But the idea of
free labor was not gender neutral. And therein lay the difficulty. For the Court, in this decision, insisted that women were
individuals within the meaning of the law and thus overturned
two decades of precedent that held that the requirements of
gender difference superseded the right to freely contract their
services. How had the two, so carefully reconciled for a generation, come into conflict?

We need to step back for a moment. Two alternative conceptions of "free labor" contested in the 1870s. The first, deriv-
ing from the early republic, had taken root in the period before
the Civil War and, by the postwar period, was championed by
such working class advocates as the Knights of Labor. In this
view, labor was free when it had the capacity to participate
independently in civic life. But that capacity inhered in the
dignity and independence of the working person and therefore
assumed that each person had equal rights or access to economic self-sufficiency. This doctrine of equal rights embodied
at least a theoretical social equality that, workers and their
representatives held, could not be sustained if workers were
reduced to permanent wage-earning status. Implicit in this
view was the notion that only economic independence could
guarantee effective self-representation and the perpetuation of

a democratic republic. The idea of free labor as it evolved in the nineteenth century thus assumed that, in order to participate effectively in the polity, workers required at least the possibility of escape from wage labor into self-directed employment.[19]

From this conception of free labor, women as individuals were virtually excluded. They were not expected to be members of the polity in the same sense as men, nor was their wage work expected to offer access to independent judgment. In the eyes of male workers women's wage labor, while dignified and offering access to self-support, ought not to lead either to independence or to self-sufficiency. Rather, just as men's free labor was predicated on their capacity to support a family, so women's was assumed to sustain the family labor of men. As family members, women participated in the polity through their menfolk. Their wage work was encouraged only in occupational fields and at moments in the life cycle that did not violate customary conceptions of free labor. For women's wage work to threaten the male's capacity to be free was a problem just as it was a problem if women's wage work undermined the capacity of either men or women to be effective family members. The American labor movement has engaged in debates on this issue since at least the 1830s, when male trade unionists protested the employment of female labor. The result of hiring women, skilled workers then thought, would be to impoverish "whole families and benefit none but the employers." They urged women to adopt strategies that would qualify them for "the more sober duties of wives, mothers and matrons."[20] The idea of free labor reified the idea of separate spheres, discouraging women from participating in wage work except in ways that would help to maintain family lives.

But labor had rules that did not necessarily derive from families. In the late nineteenth century, a dramatic acceleration in the process of industrialization threatened possibilities for self-directed employment for men as well as for women. While the defenders of free labor confronted the challenges of a debilitating and all-encompassing wage system with such innovations as cooperative producer associations and political action, a new generation of industrialists and entrepreneurs

battled them at every turn.[21] Eager for a rapid transformation
of control into their own hands and anxious to maximize the
possibilities of cheap labor, entrepreneurs treated workers as
individuals, each capable of negotiating and each protected by
the Fourteenth Amendment's prohibitions on deprivation of
property. Labor's freedom, they suggested, with the con-
currence of the courts, inhered only in its right to freely contract to sell itself.

This view, commonly known as freedom of contract, challenged labor's notions of putative social equality and threatened the economic independence from which it derived.
Within its perspective, equal rights were embedded in the
capacity of each individual to compete freely. Workers (male
and female) were free only to enter into contracts to sell their
labor without restraint. In this position entrepreneurs were
joined by the courts. As a matter of formal and legal principle,
the courts, beginning in the 1880s, ignored the vulnerable
position of workers and turned the Fourteenth Amendment's
prohibition on depriving citizens of life, liberty, and property
on its head. Consistently, they interpreted freedom of contract
as a ban on state efforts to restrict the rights of employers to
offer even the most debilitating working conditions. The
courts thus effectively snuffed the political vision of free labor.
Valiant battles of workers' organizations could not prevent this
development. With a few specific exceptions, the doctrine out-
lawed protective legislation for most workers, depriving them
of state intervention while employers were left free to impose
their own conditions of work.[22] The crack in this system was
gender.

The effort to limit labor's expectations by means of freedom
of contract expressed the stake of a rapidly industrializing
society in cheap and available labor. While theoretically, the
tendency of such a system was to pull women into the labor
force as individuals, there remained some questions as to
whether they were "protected" by the Fourteenth Amendment
as men were. For the same assault on free labor that had
undermined notions of work as the locus of dignity relied
upon, and perpetuated, the idea of the family as an economic

unit and as the source of values by which a new generation of laborers would be raised. If, on the one hand, this provided a large pool of "cheap labor," on the other, even the most hard-boiled advocates of freedom of contract could not be insensitive to the problem that women who were treated as individuals for the purpose of the workplace still needed to fulfill demanding roles as family members. Jobs that undermined the working class family by destroying women's health or fertility, or by encouraging women to compete for male jobs, could easily destroy the golden egg that produced cheap labor.

Advocates of freedom of contract differed from the champions of free labor on virtually every score. Yet both agreed to some sense of separate spheres. The content of women's roles differed for each. Labor's conception was rooted in the belief that effective civic participation demanded workplace dignity that in turn rested on an ordered and comfortable family life. Business's conception derived from the desire to preserve the family as an economic unit that could provide incentives to stable and loyal work force participation. Either way, ideas of gender difference defined women as family members whose work roles were secondary. Ideally, at least, this led to no contradiction for male workers: women, seen either as individuals who competed with them for jobs or as family members on whose household labor they relied, belonged at home. But for employers, placing women in separate spheres meant that they needed to treat women simultaneously as individuals with a sacrosanct freedom of contract and as family members in whom they and the state had a special interest. It was this contradiction that the courts were called upon to resolve in the minimum wage cases.

By 1908 they had successfully done so with regard to hours. Under pressure from coalitions of women workers, reformers, and trade unions, legislatures and courts had legitimized the now familiar device of making women "wards of the state." But what worked for hours had special consequences when applied to wages. Regulating hours, as the Court noted in Adkins, had "no necessary effect on the heart of the contract, that is, the amount of wages to be paid and received."[23] The minimum wage, in contrast, touched its core. It was designed to defend freedom of contract by ensuring that women who could not otherwise survive did not undermine an ideology that relied on the fiction of a worker's liberty to negotiate fair terms for labor. At the same time the minimum wage threatened the idea of freedom of contract by clearly identifying some workers as lacking the appropriate liberty. Tracing the resolution of this dilemma will tell us something of how ideas of gender difference help to construct social reality. For in one of the wonderful ironies of history, judicial decisions and the legal system contributed to definitions of female difference that in the end threatened the idea of the free labor market they were meant to protect.

The progressive attempt to accommodate gender invigorated a free labor debate that had been all but lost. Arguably, it helped to alter the terms of the debate. In creating sex as a category outside the common expectation of labor and law, the courts opened the door to an evaluation of the proper relation of the state to labor as a whole.[24] The language with which this struggle was enacted tells us something about the centrality of separate spheres in the lives of men and women and also about its competing functions. It enables us to watch how the notion of separate spheres first confronted and eventually helped to break down the pernicious idea of freedom of contract.

Let us begin with the case of Quong Wing, the Chinese laundry man who, in the winter of 1911-12, petitioned the United States Supreme Court for relief. Quong Wing, a male, had sued the treasurer of Lewis and Clark County, Montana, to return the $10 he had paid for a license to take in hand laundry. The Montana law, as cited by Justice Oliver Wendell Holmes in the Supreme Court decision, "imposed the payment upon all persons engaged in the laundry business, other than the steam laundry business, with a proviso that it should not apply to women so employed where not more than two women were employed."[25] Because the law applied to all laundries except steam laundries, it taxed small enterprises while exempting large ones, and because it applied to all persons who worked in hand laundries except women who worked alone or in pairs, it in effect, taxed men who did what was considered women's work. There can be little doubt that the state meant to tax Chinese men, while exempting women and large operators; for, as Justice Holmes observed in his opinion for the Court, "hand laundry work is a widespread occupation of Chinamen in this country while on the other hand it is so rare to see men of our race engaged in it that many of us would be unable to say that they had ever observed a case."[26] Yet Quong Wing did not charge racial discrimination—an issue on which Holmes thought he might well have won. Instead, he charged sexual discrimination—and lost. The Supreme Court upheld the Montana statute because, as Holmes put it,

If the state sees fit to encourage steam laundries and discourage hand laundries that is its own affair. And if again it finds a ground of distinction in sex, that is not without precedent. . . . If Montana deems it advisable to put a lighter burden upon women than upon men with regard to an employment that our people commonly regard as more appropriate for the former, the Fourteenth Amendment does not interfere by creating a fictitious equality where there is a real difference. The particular points at which that difference shall be emphasized by legislation are largely in the power of the state.[27]

This case is not the first to identify gender difference as a legal category.[28] But, unlike the rationales for restricting women's working hours, on which the Court drew and which were rooted in the presumed physical disadvantages of women and the social benefits of legislation, the Court here asserted an arbitrary power to discriminate between men and women— not a new phenomenon but one that it did not even seek to justify except as a matter of legislative choice. Quong Wing thus extended Muller's standard of sex as an appropriate classification to assert a state's right to define which sex differences could be taken into account. In imposing a new standard for legislative review, the case raises many issues, among them how readily gender "difference" is deployed under circumstances that would have explicitly precluded ethnic "difference," and the content of the "distinction" or "difference" to which the Court so blithely refers and that it makes no

attempt to define. But for our purposes the most interesting
question is the way in which the decision illuminates the social
meaning of men's and women's wages.

The decision in Quong Wing suggests that the "common
regard" (or popular perceptions of women's roles) is deter-
minative in legislative choice as to which differences shall be
emphasized. But surely that is a problem. If we take seriously
Justice Holmes's comment that "the particular points at which
that difference shall be emphasized by legislation are largely
in the power of the state," then we have little choice but to view
gender difference as an idea with a political content that
moves people to behave in certain kinds of ways—in short, as
an ideological construct. The decision tells us quite clearly
that male and female job choices, and the earnings that result,
are subject to regulation to bring them into line with the
"common regard." A look at the evidence suggests the ideological level at which gender entered the debate.

In 1912 the common regard held that women belonged in
families. Employers freely (and largely falsely) expressed the
belief that women did not need the incomes of males because
they could rely on families to support them. More subtly, in the
common regard, questions of masculinity entered into every
decision on wages. For men the wage encompassed family
support; for women it tended to incorporate only the self-
support of a single person. This was made clear by New York
State's Factory Investigating Commission of 1912. Eager to
establish a case for the minimum wage, it asked several thou-
sand employers to estimate what wage would be "required to
support in health and working efficiency" the following categories of workers:

A young woman of 16-18 years, living independently
A young man of 16 to 18 years, living independently
An adult woman living independently
An adult man living independently
A normal family containing one man at work, one woman doing her
own housework, and three children under 14 at school.[29]

No question about women supporting others was ever asked.

Rather, the opposite assumption was made, namely that it was appropriate for women to derive part of their support from families. This assumption found its way into *Adkins* where Justice Sutherland objected to the District of Columbia law because it failed to take account of "the cooperative economies of the family group, though they constitute an important consideration in estimating the cost of living, for it is obvious that the individual expense will be less in the case of a member of a family than in the case of one living alone."[30]

The wage might thus appropriately order the relations between the sexes. As a relative, not an absolute phenomenon, the wage can be read in terms of how women stretched their earnings and in terms of such larger meanings as independence or power in the family. And it can tell us something about social conceptions of womanhood and their relationship to gendered structures that extend far beyond the wage itself. How the wage "images" women—like the role it plays in fixing relationships between men and women—tells us something about how structures of difference are maintained and used. For if the common regard legitimized a lower wage for women and negated women's articulated experience about what it cost to live and help support a family, it also set the stage for the struggle over whether a minimum wage was socially desirable and economically legitimate.

Because the battle was hard fought, the price of maintaining separate spheres was high. It took the form of a vicious and clearly ideological attack on women as workers that exaggerated their "natural" attachment to the home and belittled their ability to earn wages. The popular imagination conjured up pictures of wage-earning women who were helpless, dependent, weak, handicapped, ignorant, delicate, and exploitable. Portraits of wage-earning women depicted them as greedy and lazy as well. They had, it was said, a "natural longing for recreation . . . adornment" and luxury. At the same time, women lived in a world where unscrupulous employers did not hesitate to subject them to conditions "akin to slavery" and thus leave them vulnerable to peculiar dangers that threatened to lure them into vice and immorality. These conditions prevented women from living in "decency" or from enjoying "healthy and normal lives," and they inhibited the peace of a "satisfied mind" and a "wholesome existence." Worse, they threatened the "health and well-being" of future mothers and therefore held "the strength of the nation hostage."[31] While these images expand upon those evoked to justify shorter hours for women but not for men, their consequences were not at all alike.

In the debate over the minimum wage, both sides had a stake in maintaining wage differentials, and so both resorted to this imagery. The terms of the debate thus contributed to depicting women in the extreme language of childhood and vulnerability. For example, both sides saw women as inefficient workers who lacked training. Proponents of the minimum wage argued that wage earners could be divided between those who "are earning what they receive or more" and those "whose services are worth little or nothing."[32] Even sympathetic reformers like Florence Kelley held that too many untrained and unskilled women flooding the job market depressed women's wages. To raise wages required educating and training women to be more efficient and effective workers. That this had not happened as a natural result of the market was due to defects in women's character.

Women competed with each other. Like the notion that women workers were inefficient, the idea that female competition reduced wages pervaded the imagery. One side depicted women as "undutiful daughters" who, tempted by luxurious living, allowed their mothers to overwork themselves while they sought riches in the factory or department store. Or it imagined dissatisfied wives not content to live on their husbands' earnings. Though sympathetic to the minimum wage, the other constructed a picture of "women whose earnings are supplemented from other sources" and who are therefore a "constant drag on the wage level and offer formidable competition to the growing thousands of women dependent on their own labor for support. . . ."[33] The circular logic of this argument appears when we place it in the form of a syllogism: Women do not earn enough, therefore they live with others,

therefore they reduce the level of wages for all women, therefore women do not earn enough.

Another explanation was that women chose the wrong jobs.
For example, opponents of the minimum wage suggested that
women could easily save money and achieve mobility if they
were willing to become domestic servants. Such jobs were
widely available. But women, objecting to their endless hours,
close supervision, and live-in conditions, frequently refused
them. In view of their willingness to turn down these jobs, a
minimum wage would only reinforce women's worst qualities,
rewarding the inefficient without benefiting those who were
oriented towards hard work and mobility. On the other side of
this coin, a picture of women's inability to advance themselves
could yield an argument for state aid as illustrated by the
belief that they were in occupations not reachable in the normal course of trade union organization. "A great deal can be
said for minimum wage laws and laws limiting the hours of
labor for women," asserted feminist Crystal Eastman, who
normally opposed special laws for women only, "on the ground
that women's labor is the least adapted to organization and
therefore the most easily exploited and most in need of legislative protection."[34] Women who selected jobs that restricted
their ability to bargain collectively and were, therefore, inca-
pable of securing a fair return on their wages constituted,
according to some labor leaders, "a helpless class of labor,
broken in spirit." "Practically impossible to organize under
existing conditions," they might be more readily organized
once their "broken spirit had been reinforced by a minimum
wage."[35]

Women had weak characters. Opponents of a minimum
wage suggested that legislation would increase immorality
because it would give extra money to frivolous, unworthy
people. Those who favored the minimum argued that weak
women would succumb to vice and prostitution at the least
temptation and needed higher wages to enable them to resist.[36] Neither argument seemed to have much to do with
reality. Of the fifteen experts who answered the FIC's question
as to whether women's low wages yielded prostitution, twelve

attributed prostitution to low family incomes, not the low wages of the woman worker. Still, New York's Factory Investigating Commission concluded that one of the dangers of low wages for women was vice and immorality. And a persistent demand of its nonexpert witnesses was for "a wage that a woman could live on, and live right."[37]

Public debates over the minimum wage, arguments for and against the minimum in a series of court cases, and the judicial decisions made in such cases built on these portraits. Both sides drew vivid pictures of women's helplessness in relation to work and wages in order to make a case for their positions. Those opposed to the minimum wage, and who might have relied on more complex descriptions of women's lives, chose instead to defend the wage system. Regulating the wage, in their view, would restrict the market, ignore supply and demand, reduce profits, and drive employers out of business. In the legal imagination, at least, free enterprise vied with family roles as the salvation of America. To save women might require a regulated wage; to save America required freedom of contract. The women's wage became an arena for playing out struggles that ranged far beyond domesticity.

Arguments against the minimum wage were predicated heavily on the assumption that employers paid a natural wage that was the equivalent of the service rendered—that women were worth no more than what they earned. The neoclassical economic theory on which such arguments rested held the worker responsible for his or her place in the job market. In a free market, workers who could freely sell their labor earned the economic value of what they produced. Employers hired workers at different levels of wages calculated to reflect the value of the product created as well as the supply of workers willing to accept the wages offered. If women tended to work on low-value products (garments, paper flowers, boxes, textiles, shoes, for example), that was not the employer's fault but a result of women's choices. Business could not pay more than a "natural" wage without threatening the profits that enabled it to survive. If women's wages tended to be low, the logical explanation lay in a persistent assertion of a woman's "difference." A regulated minimum that forced employers to "supply individual needs . . . in excess of what the employee earns or is worth"[38] would be disastrous. From this flowed a series of questions: Should the wage be determined not by the value of the services rendered but by the cost of supporting women? Should industry be required to cover the deficit in women's wages? Was there a constitutional question implicit in the issue of "whether an employer may be compelled to pay the cost of maintaining the employer whose full services he voluntarily uses in the conduct of an enterprise?"[39] Since no employer would stay in business without profits, would attempts to regulate wages (as a function of the cost of supporting women as opposed to the value of the services they rendered) not drive employers out?

Circumventing the idea of freedom of contract by exacerbating women's weakness and helplessness transformed the debate. Freedom of contract rested on the notion that the wage was an abstraction—the product of agreement between employer and employee. The argument over the minimum wage, because it was gendered, exposed the social issue embodied in the wage and thus kept alive a social meaning on which defenders of free labor had insisted. The Progressives connected the wage argument to hours by suggesting that if women's wages were so low as to undermine their childbearing and rearing capacities then the state as a whole would suffer because its future citizens would be weak and without good discipline and values. Under those circumstances freedom of contract would threaten the "future of the race." For the courts to accept this argument required suspending wage theory and arguing for redistribution of income according to norms of social justice that recalled the ideals of advocates of free labor.

In focusing so heavily on separate spheres, protagonists and antagonists alike begged the question of social justice in the industrial sector, evoking fears that the extreme solutions required to compensate for women's weakness might threaten the free market. Thus, the argument over wages placed the judiciary squarely in the position of deciding whether to concede separate spheres to women in order to redistribute income sufficiently for women to maintain families (granting some credence to the older free labor ideology and enabling women to keep open possibilities for gendered action) or whether to sustain freedom of contract in the face of the apparent threat to families.[40] The conundrum that this posed is revealed in the language and arguments used during the course of the debate.

First, it raised the issue of the appropriate relationship between male and female wages. If the natural wage was a male wage and women's wages were low because they "could not earn a wage," then attempts to create an arbitrary minimum for women and not for men would threaten the balance between male and female spheres. The alternative would be to raise male wages. But this begged the issue of whether a state that could impose a minimum wage could not also impose a maximum. Some who agreed that the public welfare was menaced by low wages for women had to agree that it was equally vulnerable to low male wages. For if higher wages were necessary to health and morality—if a law fixing wages was a health law—surely then it was desirable for both men and women. If benefits claimed for women were given to men after all, then whole families would benefit. As one commentator put it, "If . . . a minimum wage law for women is constitutional because it tends to provide the race with healthy moral mothers, so would a minimum wage law for men, because it would tend to provide the race with strong honest fathers."[41] Once opened, that Pandora's box could only produce a case for a higher wage for all.

Closely related to the issue of health was that of morality. One of the basic arguments for minimum wages was that women with insufficient incomes were regularly tempted into amorous relationships or even into prostitution in order to make ends meet. Raising this issue involved not only questions of male morality but those of women's character as well. As Justice Sutherland put it, "It cannot be shown that well paid women safeguard their morals more carefully than those who are poorly paid." Then he added, "If women require a minimum wage to preserve their morals, men require it to preserve their honesty."[42] The same kind of logic served the purposes of an Arkansas judge who dissented from his colleagues in believing the minimum wage to be unconstitutional. The wage, he argued, was not an issue of health and morality at all:

Wealth, at least to the extent that it affords ease and comfort, is the goal of all mankind, regardless of sex, and failure of its attainment often brings discontent and unhappiness, but I am unwilling to say that woman's health of virtue is dependent upon financial circumstances so as to justify the State in attempting to regulate her wages. Her virtue is without price in gold. She may become the victim of her misplaced affections and yield her virtue, but sell it for money—no. When she falls so low as that it is only from the isolated helplessness of her shame and degradation.[43]

If women could not earn their keep, then society, not women, would pay the cost of women's low wages. Again, women who worked were depicted as mere parasites who imposed a financial burden on the state and on other industries. Women's low wages, in this view, were nothing less than a "menace to public welfare." As Felix Frankfurter put it in the famous case of *Stettler* v. *O'Hara*, "Industries supporting male workers were being drawn upon to assist in supporting women workers engaged in other industries, which were refusing to carry their cost." Frankfurter, defending Oregon's minimum wage law, argued that the immediate effects of women's low wages were to impose financial burdens on the state, "which threatened excessive and unremunerative taxation." Women's wages, he argued, were a "community problem—a problem affecting the state in its pervasive entirety."[44]

The degree to which arguments over women's wages threatened freedom of contract emerges most forcefully in the suggestion that depictions of women's difference that fueled a demand for the minimum wage would in the end raise false expectations as to the distribution of income and property. These expectations could not, according to some, be met under the limits of the constitution, for they required "A to give part of his property to B."[45] Such an action would deny individual rights, destroy natural competition, and evoke the specter of

social revolution. Minimum wage legislation, in the words of a
June 1917 commentator, was "a new expression of the paternalistic and socialistic tendencies of the day. It savors of the
division of property between those who have and those who
have not, and the leveling of fortunes by division under govern-
mental supervision. It is consistent with the orthodox socialist
creed, but it is not consistent with the principles of our government which are based upon the protection of individual
rights."[46]

Champions of the minimum wage did not deny that individual rights were endangered by regulation. Rather, they argued
that individual rights could not be allowed to supersede the
rights of "women who must labor in order to live. It would
seem," noted Justice Wendell Stafford, who had been part of
the majority in the original D.C. Supreme Court decision that
upheld the constitutionality of minimum wages, "that the
right of this class to live on a barely decent level, and the right
of the public to have them so live, should outweigh the right of
those who do not need to work in order to live, and who
therefore are merely asserting a right to earn money and
thereby accumulate property."[47]

The idea that weak women were at some level responsible
for undermining a cherished principle of government was
echoed and expanded by court decisions at all levels beginning
in 1917. It finally became a key argument for invalidating the
minimum wage. From 1912 to 1923, the minimum wage was
more or less sustained. But by 1917 tensions provoked by the
emphasis on gender difference became apparent. Writing for
the District of Columbia Supreme Court in the penultimate
round of *Children's Hospital* v. *Adkins*, Justice Van Orsdel declared that "legislation tending to fix the prices at which private property shall be sold, . . . places a limitation upon the
distribution of wealth, and is aimed at the correction of the
inequalities of fortune which are inevitable under our form of
government, due to personal liberty and the private ownership
of property. These principles are embodied in the Constitution
itself."[48]

Imposing a minimum wage was thus the equivalent of using

the police power to "level inequalities of fortune." Van Orsdel made his own economic bias clear: "A wage based upon competitive ability is just, and leads to frugality and honest industry, and inspires an ambition to attain the highest possible efficiency, while the equal wage paralyzes ambition and promotes prodigality and indolence. It takes away the strongest incentive to human labor, thrift and efficiency, and works injustice to employee and employer alike, thus affecting injuriously the whole social and industrial fabric."[49] "No greater calamity," he continued,

could befall the wage-earners of this country than to have the legislative power to fix wages upheld. It would deprive them of the most sacred safeguard which the Constitution affords. Take from the citizen the right to freely contract and sell his labor for the highest wage which his individual skill and efficiency will command, and the laborer would be reduced to an automaton—a mere creature of the state. It is paternalism in the highest degree, . . . it is but a step to a legal requirement that the industrious, frugal, economical citizen must divide his earnings with his indolent, worthless neighbor. . . . it will logically, if persisted in, end in social disorder and revolution.[50]

Under the circumstances, to defend women's differences required what some perceived as an attack on first principles. Advocates of the minimum wage had couched their arguments in exaggerated assertions about the traditional roles of women. But to maintain those roles at the expense of freedom of contract would, in the view of a conservative judiciary, undermine the principle of individual rights and the economic system itself. To accommodate to the pressure would jeopardize the wages of men and of other women, the profits of industry, and the free enterprise system. Minimum wages, in short, would so alter the role of the state as to produce nothing less than the dreaded disease of sovietism.[51]

Faced with a sharp conflict between two ideological systems, one had to give way. If women were to continue as paid workers, the courts could either deny the importance of gender difference or negate freedom of contract. In the event, the Supreme Court chose to sustain freedom of contract by declaring the minimum wage "to be wholly beyond legislative discretion."[52] Divided 5 to 3 (with Brandeis abstaining because his daughter had been involved in preparing the brief), the Court declared that gender differences had come to the vanishing point, that there was no reason therefore to abrogate freedom of contract, and that the minimum wage was unconstitutional.

To some observers it appeared that the Court had done an "anomalous somersault." But in fact, a closer view reveals the decision to have been a logical consequence of the contradictions produced by the way in which women's differences had been incorporated into the social meaning of the wage. Speaking for the majority, Justice Sutherland evoked the underlying issues as he saw them: free enterprise was arrayed against motherhood. He concluded that free enterprise had to be preserved, even at the cost of wiping out the separate spheres. The wage, he asserted, was based on a "just equivalence of the service rendered," not on the need of the worker. No matter how pressing, the need of the worker could not avail. "The ancient inequality of the sexes," he declared in a much quoted paragraph,

has continued with diminishing intensity. In view of the great—not to say revolutionary—changes which have taken place . . . in the contractual, political, and civil status of women, culminating in the Nineteenth Amendment, it is not unreasonable to say that these differences have come almost, if not quite, to the vanishing point. . . . While the physical differences must be recognized in appropriate cases, and legislation fixing hours or conditions of work may properly take them into account, we cannot accept the doctrine that women of mature age, sui juris, require or may be subjected to restrictions upon their liberty of contract which could not lawfully be imposed in the case of men under similar circumstances.[53]

Castigating those who did not pay attention to employers' needs and acknowledging that a woman was worth little in the free labor market, he attacked the statute for failing to "require that the wage have any relation to the reasonable value of the workers' services."

Bold as the decision was, it might have been expected. It

built upon what was implicit in Holmes's opinion in Quong Wing. Holmes had there asserted that the existence of sexual difference (or separate spheres) was the legitimate province of the state to define. In his view sexual difference was a legitimate classification for legislators. By 1923, in a new political environment, the Supreme Court, stymied by the tension between attributions of gender difference and an economic system that assumed freedom of contract, chose to take the opposite position. It simply defined sexual difference out of existence.

But the issue was not so simply put to rest. The rhetoric of the debate and the reality of women's lives conspired to keep it alive. In the dissents to Adkins and in the protest that ensued, a strong appeal to social justice, rooted in family and domestic life, persisted. Dissenting Chief Justice Taft, for example, thought the majority decision unwise because "it is not the function of this court to hold Congressional acts invalid simply because they are passed to carry out economic views which the Court believes to be unwise or unsound."[54] To others it violated simple principles of social justice. "It demeans humanity," said Samuel Gompers, that "women and girl wage earners are to be bought over the counter."[55] Confusion reigned over the Court's consistent affirmation of gender difference when it came to hours and working conditions and its equally consistent opposition to sex-based classifications when wages were at stake. Case after case came to the Supreme Court, only to be turned back.[56] But by 1937 the Court once again reestablished an interest in women's difference as the opening wedge of a fight for social justice.

In *West Coast Hotel Co.* v. *Parrish*, the Court reversed itself. Chief Justice Hughes, speaking for the Court, rejected a freedom of contract defense against minimum wage legislation because, he said, "the Constitution does not speak of freedom of contract. It speaks of liberty. . . . But the liberty safeguarded is liberty in a social organization which requires the protection of law against the evils which menace the health, safety, morals and welfare of the people."[57] Speaking in the language of nineteenth century advocates of free labor, he denied any "absolute" freedom of contract and argued that liberty did not imply "immunity from reasonable regulations and prohibitions imposed in the interest of the community."[58] What were the interests of the community? They resided in protecting those parties that did not stand upon an equality and therefore in the state's interest in women.

Calling upon *Muller* v. *Oregon* and repeating the words of Quong Wing, that only a "fictitious equality" existed between men and women, the Court argued, in overturning Adkins, that women "are relatively defenseless against the denial of a living wage." Low wages were "detrimental to their health and well-being" and "cast a direct burden for their support upon the community." Echoing Holmes's insistence on the state's right to determine where difference shall be emphasized, the Court castigated selfish employers for disregarding the public interest, noted the anguish of the economic depression, and asserted that the "relative need" of women "in the presence of the evil, no less than the evil itself, is a matter for legislative judgment."[59]

But the premonitions of Van Orsdel, Sutherland, and others had not been misplaced. For though Chief Justice Hughes used gender difference to highlight the state's interest in "the exploitation of a class of workers who are in an unequal position with respect to bargaining power and are thus relatively defenseless against the denial of a living wage," he explicitly utilized female difference as the entering wedge for judicial decisions about others in need.[60] In so doing, he ensured that a new definition of liberty would prevail. Less than three years later, the Court relied on its decision in *West Coast Hotel* to sustain the constitutionality of the Fair Labor Standards Act which legislated minimum wages for men and women. But it abandoned sex difference as the crucial criterion for undermining freedom of contract. In *United States* v. *Darby,* the case that affirmed the FLSA and cleared the path for the social legislation of the modern period, the Court transcended gender and argued that "it is no longer open to question that the fixing of a minimum wage is within the legislative power."[61]

How do we explain the shift? Part of the answer lies in the

change in social conditions in the fourteen years between the two decisions. Sutherland, in dissent from the majority in *West Coast Hotel*, tried once again to make the case that there was no longer any reason why women "should be put in different classes in respect of their legal right to make contracts. Nor should they be denied, in effect, the right to compete with men for work paying lower wages which men may be willing to accept."[62] This argument carried little weight in the depression climate. But much of the shift in Court opinion lies in the way that language about women and agitation around them had demonstrated the evident social purposes of such legislation. By the 1930s, when public opinion was once again ready to consider the search for social justice as part of the legitimate end of government, the idea that women constituted a separate and deserving class could and did serve to illustrate the rigidity of old doctrines of freedom of contract. Attention to gender differences had kept alive the possibility that all workers deserved state protection. As Justice Stone put it in his dissent from the Court's final attempt to preserve the sanctity of freedom of contract in *Morehead* v. *New York*, "In the years which have intervened since the Adkins case . . . we have had opportunity to perceive more clearly that a wage insufficient to support the worker does not visit its consequences upon him alone; that it may affect profoundly the entire economic structure of society and, in any case, that it casts on every taxpayer, and on government itself, the burden of solving the problems of poverty, subsistence, health and morals of large numbers in the community."[63]

Looking at the struggle over the minimum wage should convince us that, whatever the realities of gender differences, the idea of difference constitutes at least part of the cultural context within which debates over workplace aspirations and expectations are shaped. As difference remains embedded in the wage, so it is hidden in other arenas of social policy. But, in the progressive period, gendered ideas contested with other systems of thought to produce the compromises that yielded familiar legislation. If we think about legislation this way, we might learn something about how ideas are institutionalized into law and public policy. For as Justice Holmes put it in 1912, "the particular points at which [sex] difference shall be emphasized by legislation are largely in the power of the state." Whether we agree with them or not, the Progressives fully understood and utilized that idea.

3. Providers
An Exploration of Gender Ideology in the 1930s

There are a lot of other boys and girls out of jobs now.
There are lots of women who are working in the mills
who have husbands working every day, and the men are
making enough money to support them. Why not get
these women out of the mills and give the young girls a
chance. There are a lot of women working just for
pleasure and for cars. Why not stop all of that and give
the girls who really need the work to pay for board and
clothes a chance.

—Mother of four girls, all jobless[1]

On May 10, 1933, Earl Leiby of Akron, Ohio, wrote to Franklin
Delano Roosevelt, president of the United States:

You are probably aware of the fact that homes are being wrecked daily
due to the fact that married women are permitted to work in factories
and offices in this land of ours. You and we all know that the place for a
wife and mother is at home, her palace. The excuse is often brought up
that the husband cannot find employment. It is the writers' belief that
if the women were expelled from places of business, . . . these very
men would find employment. These same women's husbands would
naturally be paid a higher salary, inasmuch as male employees demand a higher salary than females.[2]

Like other people who chose the early months of a new administration to pass on suggestions for relief to the president, Mr.
Leiby was convinced that the solution to three long years of
economic depression lay in a return to old values. For him, as
for others, a restoration of women and men to their appropri-

ate spheres would return peace and prosperity to the land. But if Leiby's belief in a particular form of domesticity was widespread, it was not universal.

Consider the following letter from Mrs. Blanche Crumbly, a weaver of McDonough, Georgia, who wrote to FDR on October 26, 1933. The letter, written in pencil on lined foolscap paper, protested the failure of her textile mill employers to pay her an expected $12 a week. "I am sending you my checks to show you what I made," she wrote.

I want to let you see that they didn't pay me enough. I worked eight hours a day and you will see they have me marked up forty hours a week and didn't pay twelve dollars and by law they were supposed to pay twelve dollars whether you operated one machine or not but I worked in the weave shop and run five looms so I want you to see that I get my money that is due me for I am just a poor woman and was working trying to make some money but they didn't pay enough to keep me working so I want you to write right back to me and let me know what you can do.[3]

Nothing in this letter speaks to the values of domesticity. If the subtext has the ring of humility, the message is insistent and demanding. Mrs. Crumbly wants action, not on the basis of her place in the household, but as a matter of workplace justice. She had worked in the weave shop running five looms; she had earned her pay; she was a poor woman who needed the money.

These letters seem to reflect opposing positions on the issue of domesticity: the first assumes its inevitability and explicitly validates it; the second fails even to acknowledge its existence, much less its role in shaping the labor force. From the perspective of the first letter writer, the world appears to be structured around the household whose effective regulation would have a salutary effect on the economy. In that of the second, work and wages are central—their just resolution by state agencies is demanded independently of the writer's household role. Taken together, these letters raise questions about the validity of the notion of separate spheres—a notion that has dominated American women's history for the past two decades.

Traditionally, "separate spheres" connotes a middle class world of privatized households in which women, excluded from the public arena, protect the values associated with morality and virtue and nurture against a competitive, aggressive, and individualistic world. Historians who first perceived separate spheres as an ideology adopted by women to justify their exclusion from public life and to rationalize the effects of an economy that increasingly removed production from the household have, more recently, seen in the idea the capacity of women to create networks of female power and access routes to political influence.[4] In that appealing form, the values engendered by domesticity, which constitute the core of separate spheres, have moved far beyond their original boundaries. Stretched across class lines and now widely applied to analyses of poor, black, and immigrant women, the idea of separate spheres underlines female participation in, and control of, neighborhood activity. It is used, for example, to illuminate the emergence of spontaneous protests against rising prices for bread, meat, and rents, as well as to explain how cross-class alliances are sustained.[5] Thus, the notion of separate spheres, which once suggested the limits of family life, is now offered as the most important source of female power.

If the major contribution of separate spheres as a historical construct has been to allow us to evaluate women on their own terms, what are we to make of those women—wage-earning women—who demonstrably functioned in the male-dominated world of paid labor on a daily basis? The idea of separate spheres requires us as historians to attribute to women a conception of identity that is primarily gender based (rooted, that is, in the things that women primarily do). This might accurately reflect the self-images of those whose lives were undivided between family and paid work, but it is problematic for the vast majority whose daily existence straddled both arenas. And it raises questions we have not yet learned how to pose. To what extent do historically specific circumstances define a gendered identity? As the nineteenth century gave way to the twentieth, can we still argue that, whatever its validity among privileged women who lived in a predominantly commercial setting in the 1820s, domestic values continue to reflect the daily lives of most women? And what of men? Are we willing to argue that their identity, too, though rooted in the world of work, is gender based? If so, then the social construction of gender must become a central problematic of social history whose role in such processes as class formation will require careful analysis. For the moment, however, I pose a simpler question: does gender adequately reflect the ways that ordinary women and men self-identify in a given historical period or at a given phase of their lives?

Because the concept of separate spheres rests on assumptions not only about the centrality of gender identity but about its dichotomous nature, historians have already begun to challenge it. In particular, Linda Kerber has noted the ways in which it has grown to encompass all of the triptych represented by women-home-family and has become interchangeable with each of them. Almost unwittingly, the notion has entered into the language of the historical profession, acting as a metaphor that has "helped historians to select what to study and how to report what they found.[6] When Nancy Hewitt attempted to pull the metaphor apart and examine its meaning, she discovered that it created a fundamentally distorted picture of sisterhood and bonding across class and race lines. The reality, she argued, was quite other. Women might have bonded within ethnic, racial, and class groups; but, far from facilitating unity among all women, these bonds tended to serve as barriers to it.[7]

In warning us to distinguish the historian's usages of separate spheres from the capacity of the idea to represent reality and in suggesting that the idea has no universal definition, this work alerts us to the degree of romanticism that has crept into our visions of women's lives.[8] It raises a third set of issues that revolve around the social meanings embodied in the idea of separate spheres as they are incorporated into the language of historians and used to describe the life-styles of different groups of people. On the surface the concept appears to be quintessentially feminist. It avoids conventional hierarchical assumptions about men and women by exploring and evaluating female behavior in a context created by women. But, in fact, because it is a model that rests on social and cultural perceptions of gender difference, its operation depends on constructing another (public/male/work) sphere against which the female sphere can be measured. Though the boundaries of the two are permeable, in making gender difference the pivot of the analysis of political and social behavior, the model nevertheless builds dichotomous and sometimes oppositional categories into our language and our interpretations.[9] It constructs, for example, normative standards of behavior that are either male or female; it conjures up conceptions of right and wrong that differ for men and women. In so far as difference is inevitably hierarchical, the conception of separate spheres perpetuates, instead of undermining, hierarchical patterns of thought.

While appearing to be a feminist perspective, then, the idea of separate spheres affirms inequality on three levels. In the first instance, it elevates the reality of bonding along gendered lines above all other forms of connectedness. In the second, it organizes historical data in a way that emphasizes potential inequalities, rather than seeking commonalities. And, finally, it inhibits our capacity as historians to conceive modes of thought and behavior that contain nonoppositional or non-dichotomous possibilities.

Given the existence of domestic life for most women in the United States in the nineteenth and twentieth centuries, it would be difficult to think about the past in relationship to women without resorting to some notion of domesticity that is derived from separate spheres. By avoiding dichotomized notions, however, we might be able to remove it from the center of our analysis, retaining domesticity as a category of behavior and a source of values that has had an important (but not universally defining) effect on the lives of women and men. Such an approach would avoid the confining and historically problematic connotations of separate spheres while retaining the possibilities of domesticity as a strategic mode and as one aspect of the diversity that encompasses women's lives.

Consider, for example, what happens when we try to rethink the lives of wage-earning women from their own perspectives. The sexual division of labor is widely, and I think correctly, assumed to rest on social conceptions of appropriate male and female work inside and outside the household. These legitimate the prevailing economic system by rationalizing inequality between men and women. But because the sources of these conceptions are seen as oppositional (men and women have different needs of and requirements in the work force), and thus self-reinforcing, they have obscured the extent to which other processes, like industrialization, suburbanization, and the advent of a consumer society, have utilized and perpetuated gendered ideologies. In the labor market, enormous efforts had to be made to maintain boundaries that defied the immediate economic self-interest of employers and female employees and arguably, at least, of male workers in their capacity as husbands and fathers as well. These efforts transcended class lines. To put it another way, the economic inefficiency that frequently defined the sexual division of labor was sustained only by an ideological conviction (and it was no less than ideological) that the separate spheres were naturally ordained.[10] A competing paradigm might have explored how industrial development (or suburbanization, or the advent of a consumer society) altered the gendered expectations with which men and women entered the labor force.

Lacking that competing paradigm, historians of women's work have tended to discuss work in relation to the home. Although the results range widely, they have in common an emphasis on the home as the place where female values around both paid work and family life are nurtured. They include Leslie Tentler's efforts to see in the early twentieth century sweatshop and factory a reinforcement of custom and tradition that is rooted in domestic life. They stretch to the work of Susan Benson and Barbara Melosh who portray a female culture in the department store and hospital that reflects women's efforts to utilize domestic values in workplace situations in order to influence their working conditions. And they include as well as my own attempts to demonstrate that domestic values and workplace opportunity act in dialectic relationship, the one utilizing and building on the other until an inevitable contradiction shifts the balance in the other direction.[11] Whatever the particular interpretation, because we have operated from the assumption that the feet of the women we study have been firmly planted in a domestic sphere, we have had to come to terms with that first. The result has been a picture of wage-earning women who confronted the difficulties of maintaining domestic values and behavior at home while fighting for "equality" at work—whatever equality meant in a given historical period.

In all of this work, the domestic sphere is viewed as analytically separable from, and sometimes in practice separated from, what goes on at work. There are two spheres. Women and men may function in both, but gender (qualified by race and class) defines the source of one's active identity. The device has been useful in explaining woman's disadvantaged positions in the work force as a function of the gender system in which she operates. But, in the end, it serves as both a justification of female behavior and as an explanation of its consequences. It justifies the failure to make common cause across gender lines. It explains the consequences in terms of home attachments and attitudes. And it carries the ring of inevitable repetition since it offers up a picture of a female work culture that relies heavily on women's own values to identify acceptable parameters of female behavior and to order work force expectations and responses. We have produced a self-confirming cycle. If, for example, the data revealed women to have organized themselves to exercise some control over their daily working lives and resist excessive workplace demands, we, as historians, looked for ways in which their behavior affirmed domesticity. We noted how women had demonstrated the strength of community or brought behavior patterns and skills derived from the household into the workplace. We pointed to the "safe spaces" women had created at work. But we did not ask how and whether they had altered the structure of power. If the data revealed female workers to have organized in single-sex locals, we, as historians, conditioned by the perspective of separate spheres, evaluated their internal dynamics, stressed their isolated positions within the labor movement, and noted their ephemeral nature.[12]

The idea of female domesticity thus appears as both a description of the ideology that governed, or attempted to govern, the lives of some women and men and as a lens through which we have viewed the construction of gender. But is it the lens through which female workers viewed their world? Is it the only lens? Or even the most important one? Recent historical work suggests that the visual frames through which ordinary people viewed their worlds may in fact have been much more complex. For example, Sue Cobble points out that waitresses in the 1920s and 1930s fought for the right to serve alcoholic beverages at night—a job they had customarily been denied. They took this position without challenging male control of other jobs or the male prerogative of greater pay. But, Cobble concludes, waitresses' attitudes did not come out of respect for male responsibility or a sense of the limits of their own "sphere." Rather, they were a product of a realistic effort to maximize their incomes without jeopardizing job security.[13] Such an orientation, based on work-related consciousness rather than on domestic concerns, may have been typical of female workers who did not believe their work status was temporary. Similarly, Mary Blewett, discussing female shoe workers in the mid nineteenth century, notes that work orientations differ in relation to women's relationship to the work process as well as in relation to the family. Workers who were unmarried and skilled evolved arguments for free labor that placed them in alliance with skilled men and in conflict with married women homeworkers.[14]

Together, these suggest a notion of what Carole Turbin has called "nondichotomous" differences—differences that are not so sharp as to be mutually exclusive and whose boundaries realign themselves as a result of circumstance.[15] From this perspective gender or the cognitive aspects of a male or female sense of self form only one element of the way women or men perceive and structure their relationships to work. It provides one of the facets, but not the sole determinant, of what Charles Sabel would call a world view. Sabel's formulation of a worker's "career at work" acknowledges "that different work groups have different ideas of success . . . that they differ about which powers define dignity, which jobs count as disgraces and which as accomplishments." The choices made at work thus become, in Sabel's words, "a compressed cosmology that defines what virtue is and how to test it."[16] That cosmology emerges from and extends beyond work. It is revealed in workers' ideas about which jobs are acceptable, which are violations of custom, and which are intolerable. At the same time, it acknowledges the likelihood that one individual may have several sometimes competing "world views" or orientations. This perspective opens the door for a gender-neutral understanding of work, one that challenges the twin assumptions that men's ideas about work can be understood as a function of their relationships to the workplace while women's world views are uniquely derived from the domestic realm and continue to shape their behavior in the arena of paid employment.

These competing world views are held together in an interpretative framework derived from an individual's gendered experience in society with social groups and institutions.[17] The pieces that make up a coherent perspective are processed through different cognitive and social sieves. Gender and race are surely among the most important ways of sifting experience in the American context. And yet people from apparently similar circumstances may take entirely different courses of action. So the psychology, culture, ideology, and tradition that filter understanding are crucial. But so, too, are workplace experiences as they interact with one's place in the life cycle. Together, these changing and interactive constructs tell us something about the coherent conception of justice on which an individual will act.

If domestic values do not alone constitute the total explanation of how women enter into, and behave in, the work force, they, along with class and race, certainly constitute a piece of an individual's world view. How those pieces function in the construction of a consciousness that leads to action is not independent of historical circumstance. Since American historians discovered Edward Thompson's *Making of the English Working Class* in the late 1960s, they have been guided by the idea that the history of workers must honor indigenous conceptions of justice or dignity. In its simplest form, Thompson has imparted the idea that working people possess a sense of justice rooted in tradition and custom and that these elements modify an abstract conception of class. Whatever its weaknesses, the Thompsonian insistence on incorporating historical process into otherwise abstract notions of class has opened the door to including gendered perceptions as well in any discussion of the ways in which ordinary people confronted and ordered their worlds.[18]

In the light of Thompsonian insights, it remains puzzling why the language that defines the workplace has remained so obstinately male and why metaphors of domesticity have played so little role in interpretations of a male sense of justice or dignity. For example, David Montgomery's notion of manliness captures a sense of how male workers resisted encroachments on their rights as workers, ordered the workplace, and fought to maintain control of the work process.[19] In his work and that of other historians, male resistance is captured in control over time as in the printer's celebrated capacity to drink in the afternoons or the southern textile worker's willingness to take days off to go hunting. It appears as well in the geographical mobility available in some crafts and the time-honored custom of appropriating one's daily quotient of free cigars.[20] But what of female resistance? We can identify comparable female successes in, for example, women's capacity to negotiate time to nurse babies, wash laundry, or prepare the weekend meals. Yet this is frequently defined by male co-workers and by employers as docility.[21] Nor is it treated by most historians as the assertion of familial needs that constitutes at least part of its motivation. Not accidentally, then, such notions as "manliness" and brotherhood among union members appear as synonyms for strength and solidarity in the face of employer attacks, while behavior that is affirmed and sustained by association with domesticity is treated as detrimental to effective collective resistance. In fact, the historical record suggests the value of such behavior for community solidarity and increasingly calls into question notions of identity and consciousness for men and women that derive primarily from workplace conditions.[22] While wage-earning women have frequently behaved in "manly" ways and some historians have suggested that female workers often adhere to goals like the stint that are more characteristic of men, the routine behavior of male and female workers is sharply distinguished and differently assessed. Most historians continue to rely on a dichotomized model of sexual difference to explain workplace behavior.

But suppose one switched gears and tried to think about what gender meant in the lives of working people—searching as Sally Alexander has suggested for their subjective experience.[23] Suppose we crossed what Linda Kerber called the boundaries of hermeneutics and asked not "What is the meaning of work?" or "What gendered images does it construct?" but "How is work interpreted by those who do it?" or "how have the orientations of observers shaped the boundaries with which we conceive the work of others?" Such an approach might give us the opportunity to explore how gendered images function in ways that respect the constraints of such crucial factors as race and class. We take our cue, then, from the methods of Foucault who suggests that destabilizing the language with which we describe experience may in fact tell us something of the experience itself. And we attempt to understand difference, not as a single necessary dichotomy, but as a set of intersecting circles of experience that together structure consciousness.

The depression of the 1930s provides an ideal place to examine this question because its atypicality opens working people's world views to public examination. The previous decade had witnessed a dramatic rise in the proportion of married workers among wage-earning women, heightening public concern about the breakdown of the traditional family among some sectors while encouraging others to claim that female wage work helped hold families together.[24] Increased concern preceded and was sharply exacerbated by a fearsome and rising tide of unemployment that engulfed the country beginning in the winter of 1929. In the period between the election of FDR in November 1932 and his inauguration four months later, nearly a quarter of the labor force was unemployed, and emergency conditions prevailed everywhere. The result was an unprecedented discussion of who was and was not entitled to work.

One of the nation's first and most immediate responses was to exclude the spouses of wage earners from the labor force. Pressure was brought on employers to fire married women; states passed laws discriminating against married women teachers; and the federal government responded by passing section 232 of the National Economy Act, which allowed only one partner in a marriage to draw a federal salary.[25] But though public pressure continued, neither the numbers nor the proportion of married women working declined in response. We now understand this to have been a function of the desperate straits in which families found themselves when they were driven from the land, or when the traditional breadwinner, generally male, lost his job or was reduced to a few hours a week of work. As family need pushed women into the labor market, they were simultaneously pulled by a segregated labor market whose aggregate demand for female workers recovered more quickly than for males. The result was that women who needed to support families in whole or part either continued to work or went out to work for the first time.[26] Self-evident need, however seemed invisible to many.

So great was sentiment against married women holding jobs that it provoked hundreds of letters to President Roosevelt, Eleanor Roosevelt, the National Recovery Administration code authorities, Secretary of Labor Frances Perkins, and the Women's Bureau of the Department of Labor. Beginning in 1932 and reaching a crescendo in the spring of 1933, writers suggested that married women with employed husbands had no right to work and ought to be forcibly ejected from jobs. The letters came from single and married women, from widows, and from men of all kinds. Many were nearly illiterate. Most were handwritten, sometimes in pencil. Some were written on the letterheads of apparently prosperous businesses, others on foolscap. They complained of injustices done, asked for help, and offered solutions to the depression crisis.

My reading of these letters is not scientific in any sense. It could not be, for the letters themselves represent no known sample of the population, and the context that motivated them is often obscure. Moreover, they were frequently passed from office to office. A letter addressed to the president might end up in the files of the NRA; one written to Frances Perkins was quite likely to be sent on to the Women's Bureau. Nonetheless, they offer a spectacular opportunity to explore the meanings of work as they appear in a spontaneous outburst. The letters tell us about much more than gendered responses under emergency conditions. They speak to a sense of social order that is much more consistent than the contradictions implied by a superficial reading. Read carefully and together, they illuminate a moral code that transcends gendered identification and simultaneously affirms it.

In the lexicon of separate spheres, these letters appear at first to reflect the significance of that concept in the daily lives of their authors, though they offer no immediately apparent distinctions between those written by men and women. Many of both sexes insist, like Earl Leiby, on "a woman's place," suggesting that the historian's interpretation and the common wisdom were not far apart. "Have all women stop working," wrote an East St. Louis, Illinois, resident. "Put them back in their homes where they belong and then there would not be enough men to fill the jobs. Then we would have better homes, more children, a more contented people, and a better place to live in every way."[27] "The panic will be over," suggested an insurance agent from Kansas City, Missouri, "when and only when women no longer have to work . . . or . . . when men again become *men* and provide for their mothers, sisters, wives and daughters, and womanhood is again restored to its pedestal motherhood of the yesterday and man to the manhood of the yesterday."[28] Such perceptions are not gender specific. Miss B. Wohlmaker of Brooklyn wrote to Franklin Delano Roosevelt, "I have heard so much about prosperity. I don't think it will ever return as long as married women are taking the Bread and Butter out of the men who have familys to support."[29]

The common wisdom, then, is that women have a primary domestic role while men are responsible for earning their family's living. These letters have been used by historians to affirm the value of such a notion in framing the history of women and in making a case for the ideological hegemony of domesticity whether or not men and women could always adhere to its precepts in their own lives. But a closer examination reveals that the domestic role is far from a separate sphere. Concerns over both work and family life converged in a widely shared conception of justice that neither contradicted a felt perception of role difference nor entirely depended on it. Rather, images of justice seem to have been shaped by the impact of the material world. The letters reveal an integration of wage work and family life that belies the dualistic paradigms of work and domesticity typically utilized by historians. They present instead a perception of social reality far more unified than that embodied within a notion of separate spheres.

The first thing revealed by these letters is the sharp distinction made by those who believed work to be an individual right and the vast majority who did not. Women who pleaded for their jobs or angrily declared their rights to have been violated tended to claim rights as citizens. Thus, twenty-eight married women dismissed by New York State after thirteen or more years in civil service jobs protested the injustice "of depriving us as individuals of our right to security under the Civil Service Law."[30] A June 1932 petition from the Texas Federation of Business and Professional Women repeated the point: "We do not believe this country has reached the point where it is willing to be sovietized, and to have employment granted or denied as a dole."[31] The point was simply made as the female

assistant postmaster of Deerfield, Michigan, wrote to Frances
Perkins: "I can't see why if we women are American Citizens
why we haven't just as much right to work as anybody. I would
have written to the Post Master General but woman to woman
I thought you would understand better."[32]

A predepression world of job opportunity, where ambition
might be rewarded, could afford to make room for personal
goals for both men and women. Such sentiments, undoubtedly
deeply felt and more extensive than the records show, continued to be expressed among the better off. In the depression
world, the concept that a job was a right of citizenship appeared to be selfish. It was not characteristic of either the
working or the nonworking poor before or after the depression.
In contrast to the official stance of the Department of Labor
under Frances Perkins and of the Women's Bureau, most of
those who put pen and pencil to paper did so to argue that
work was the prerogative of those who needed to support
themselves and their families. In the code of honor of working
people, jobs belonged to providers.[33] Though this typically
meant married men, the scales of justice encompassed widows, single women, and married women with unemployed or
disabled husbands as well. And while ambivalence reigned
about the rights of single men, males with other means of
support were clearly excluded. As one writer explained the
priorities, "The idea is to first place to work all men who have
dependents, then girls who have dependents. The remaining
jobs to be given to those not having dependents."[34]

The idea appeared to be self-evident because it did not begin
with the depression. Such comments affirm ideas of justice
among the working poor that certainly antedate economic
crisis. Those who continued to work, like Blanche Crumbly,
clearly thought of themselves as providers. Their work was
part of a long tradition in which wages were seen as part of
their contribution to family well-being. As the Women's Bureau of the Department of Labor put it in 1924, married women worked "for one purpose and generally speaking, for one
purpose only—to provide necessities for their families or to
raise their standard of living."[35] Among communities of textile

workers in the South and among some immigrant women in
the North, wage work for wives had long been part of a pattern
of shared family support. Thus, one New Hampshire textile
worker told an interviewer that she, not her husband, had been
the first to return to work after a 1922 strike. She offered two
reasons. First, "fall was coming and we didn't have any money.
We didn't know how we were going to live." Second, "I was
afraid he would be hurt by the pickets."[36] During the depression women like this resisted removal from the work force, not
out of ideological commitment, but because they clearly did
not feel themselves to be the selfish, neglectful women described in many of the letters.

Such tacit acknowledgment of shared responsibility enables us to make sense of the general hostility that surrounded
married women's work while it simultaneously explains how a
Blanche Crumbly functioned outside the orbit of apparently
traditional roles. The role of provider served to legitimate the
roles of women, married and single, who earned wages; but it
did not prevent them from being turned into targets by those
men and women who perceived married women as unfair
competitors. Single women, widowed and divorced mothers,
and the wives of unemployed workers constituted a large proportion of the cacophonous complainants.

Indeed, other women were often the most virulent advocates of removing married women from jobs. Identifying not
with their sex but with their work/family positions, they complained on behalf of others like them. "How can the youth of
our land eliminate married women from working and taking
from us every means of support, every hope, every chance for
morality and high standards?" asked a young, single woman
from Bellingham, Washington.[37] "If there were not so many
married women working who have husbands working and no
family, we single women might stand a better show in getting a
job," wrote another.[38] A mother from Redonda [sic] Beach,
California, asserted, "It keeps our Boys and Girls from getting
work and they are the ones that need it."[39] And Lorena Ankron
of Pawhuska, Oklahoma, wanted to oust married women with
"husbands who have good jobs" because "widow women with

children should have this kind of work."[40] Widow women did not fail to assert their provider roles in justification of a demand for a job. One textile worker, fired because she was unable to make the minimum rate of production, pleaded for her job back: "I am a widow with one child to support with no job no fuel and no provision and House Rent to pay."[41]

If women self-identified not only as women but as young people, family supporters, parents, and dependents, they were vulnerable to any who threatened their family lives, whether such people were male or female. Men and women translated their sense of grievance to all who seemed to undermine the provider role, including most especially farmers, country people, anyone who did not live in their town, foreigners, and nameless racketeers. The free-flowing relationships of these categories appears in the following letter to Frances Perkins. After first insisting that married women ought to "be compelled by law to give up their positions to single girls and married men," the writer went on to complain about foreigners along with married women holding "most of our city and country positions and consuming 90% of the welfare money."[42] In other words, males who had other means of support faced the same criticism as married women. This was especially true in communities (like the textile mills of the Piedmont) where family wage work was the norm rather than the exception. L.A. Cook, a fixer at the Cannon mills in Concord, North Carolina, complained to Gen. Hugh Johnson, chief of the National Recovery Administration, "about so many farmers working in the mill a farmer will come by they will hire them before they will an experienced hand they make their crops raise most of what they eat lights water, rent not costing anything when people here in town cant get jobs . . . the way it is the farmer is holding a job down here and farming too."[43] The complaint is echoed by female mill workers such as Mrs. Lee A. Crayton, a twelve-year veteran of the Cannon mills: "Our greatest obstacle though, at the present time is the country people. They come to the Textile mills in the winter and work for less money than the people in the city can afford to work for as the country man owns his home, raises practically all of his groceries. He can afford to work for less money than the people in the city who has to depend on the textile mills for their living."[44]

At issue here is a question broader than gender but in which gender participates and to some extent becomes the scapegoat. A careful reading of these letters suggests that while the perspective of domesticity was certainly an available angle of vision, it was not the only perspective that guided the attack on married women workers. Where, then, is the outrage rooted? The privileges of relative affluence seemed to negate a shared sense of social justice rooted in the family. Whether such affluence stemmed from a gendered role or in farm ownership, it sparked outrage when it prevented those with greater need from earning a living. The resulting anger can hardly be attributed to false consciousness. More accurate, I think, would be to see the outrage as a violation of expectations about the work/household nexus. For the men and women who complained that jobs were going to the undeserving, conceptions of dignity did not lie in equal opportunity, or in equality, but rather in the intertwined reality of their own complex images of themselves and in their expectations of family life.

At one level what was at issue was whether the free market (which gave employers the prerogative of hiring most cheaply) would prevail over indigenous standards of justice. This is apparent in the various levels of exasperation with which writers asked why the government couldn't take control of the situation. "Why not issue an order that all married women whose husbands are employed be dropped from payrolls? Why not issue an order that all men drawing retired pay be dropped from payrolls?" read one letter to Hugh Johnson in its entirety.[45] Another letter writer asked of the president, "Why can't you forbid these great corporations and all others with few exceptions employing women to do men's work."[46] A third insisted that "any man that can issue a proclamation to close all the banks in the United States" could certainly issue a proclamation banning women from working for wages.[47] Whether leveled at government, at employers, or at workers, these queries reflected impatience with the failure of those in power to understand their perspective. Freedom of choice and free enterprise were clearly not the major concerns of most letter-writers. A Liberty, Missouri, man touched the core when he asked whether the employers of working women were living up to the NRA: "I can see no justice in their practices and many of the good citizens of this town are of the same opinion."[48] And many wondered with the woman from Redonda Beach why "when big Co of any kind begin Ecommizing they start on the Poor man that is just making a living in the first place. I think theire should be something done about that."[49]

Behind the frequent complaints of writers that they, or someone they knew, had been fired and replaced by someone who would work for less lay a conviction that family values had somehow been ignored or forgotten. "Did it ever occur to you," asked a Swansea, Massachusetts, resident, "the number of husbands and wives who are employed and receiving a revenue . . . my idea is that just one in a family namely either man or wife should be employed."[50] A self-described "business girl" who had lost her job asked for the removal of women with external support such as "married women and home girls" who were, she argued, "inefficiently taking the place of some man or efficient business girl as they are working for a lower salary."[51] The meaning of efficiency to her is clear: Like most of the letter writers, she found incomprehensible the government's refusal to act to change a system that appeared so patently unfair.

In expressing their skepticism about the capacity of the market to sustain what seemed to be elementary notions of justice, writers conflated public and private spheres. Indeed, one of the most striking things about these letters is their consistent inability or unwillingness to separate the two. The family may have been the private domain of individuals, but male and female workers interpreted its survival and protection as a public duty. In a situation such as the depression, the most intimate details of one's life became a public issue; the idea of a distinct domestic sphere scarcely existed. Most letter writers translated work into wages—wages that held the capacity to sustain or undermine the moral precepts thought to reside in the family. Thus, the income produced by work constituted the glue that melded the family, that joined public and private together. Like some modern epoxies, it had to be mixed just right.

While few doubted that only an adequate income could preserve family values, most correspondents feared that an income that was either too low or too high would yield moral disaster for the individual, the family, and the community as a whole. They spoke of "necessity" wages as opposed to "luxury" wages. Depriving families of the first—the result of allowing the wrong people to hold jobs—would yield moral degeneration. It encouraged the "less strong in character" to spend their time "loafing and resorting to crime for a living"[52] and reduced them to "standing on the street corners planning to rob someone."[53] It could result in "deplorable conditions, moral issues with which we are constantly confronted"[54] like "forcing many young girls on the streets because they have to get along the best they can."[55]

But the relatively high income—the luxury wage—of the dual income family was perceived as no less threatening to an individual's character and equally responsible for private and public moral degeneration. "All over the country," wrote a self-described "unemployed young woman," "women marry and immediately return to their jobs, instead of endeavoring to live within their husband's income and living a domesticated life, building a home, etc."[56] Even worse, "The women consistently dodge motherhood and go home after their work is done with a paper carton in one hand and a can opener in the other."[57]

If the immediate consequences of imbalanced income were private, everyone understood the ultimate social cost. Fears that such behavior would undermine the moral character of the nation as a whole emerged in the comments of an unemployed male office worker from Englewood, Colorado, who was replaced by the wife of a "salesman who makes a good salary": "And she and her husband purchased a new auto, and then hired help in their home so that their two children could go around the streets and grow up and not be reared by parents personally as they should but they should worry if their children would grow up to become candidates for houses of correction."[58] While the maldistribution of jobs could cause degeneration of the moral fiber of the family and therefore of the nation, so, too, could it distort the economic priorities of the nation's families. Despite the poverty and deprivation that drove most women to seek paid employment, in the public mind women's wages did not buy the same things as men's wages. Distinctions between how men and women were thought to spend their incomes exacerbated public concern about the nation's future. A male who worked would, in the popular parlance, "spend his income to the support of his family while the woman spends for permanent waves, lip sticks. But those things do not pay the grocer and all the other bills that father is expected to pay walking up and down the street looking and praying for something to do. The woman comes home says she works for her money and she will do as she pleases with it which is a fact."[59] If a boy gets a job, "he marries, buys a home, a car, a radio, etc. But a girl—its cosmetics and finery, the loss often of modesty and refinement, drifting farther and farther from matrimony, in most cases."[60]

Distinctions about what the wage was likely to buy constituted the easiest way of determining what was fair. A wage ought not to be frittered away on luxuries while its absence prevented others from sustaining the provider role. As a Washington, D.C. lawyer put it, "I do not believe these women are making as good use of the money they receive as would be made of it if it was paid to the husbands of other women who are desperately in need of employment and whose wives are staying at home looking after the home and children."[61] But the sentiment was not male alone. A single woman wrote that she knew of "any number of married women who work just in order that they might have fine furniture, clothes and a nice automobile, while we single women must go without the necessities of life."[62] She was joined by another who complained that in families with two earners "many of the married couples pay no taxes, live in rented quarters, spend their money on nice clothes, fine cars and a general 'good time.' "[63]

Encoded in these comments is the sense that the individual rights to which the ideology of a free labor market theoretically entitled all workers were not, in practice, available to some. But nobody took the ideology to task. Neither the realities of the segregated labor market, nor the economic desperation that drove most of those who sought jobs, protected wage-earning married women. They were blamed for acting unfairly. They were taking jobs from men and from single women; they were destroying the moral fiber of men and reducing men's respect for women. They were responsible for the delinquency of children and for the disintegration of the family. The continuing depression was laid at their feet—the future of the nation placed in their hands. These messages, as the letters convey, were deeply held and virulently argued. They mitigated against a continuing demand for female equality and help to explain why the assertion of individual rights, which brought the nation to such a pass, appears to be unfair.

Public opinion contrasted sharply with the responses of government representatives that, even when they acknowledged the legitimacy of the search for justice, repeatedly affirmed the role of the free market. Typically, A.R. Forbush, chief of the Correspondence Division of the NRA, replied to complainants, "It is not a function of the National Recovery Administration to tell an employer whom he may or may not employ."[64] But Forbush added the wish that employers might police themselves. "An ideal solution would be an investigation on the part of the employer of all applications for jobs and then the giving of work to those most in need."

Many of the married women who earned wages would not have disagreed with these sentiments. Understanding their self-image as providers should give us some insight into workplace behavior, into the sense of justice on which women will act. If the provider role was central, then the failure of employers to live by it would yield tension. Mrs. Blanche Crumbly protested the insufficient $12 a week, but she quit because "they didn't pay enough to keep me working." A year or two later, under other circumstances, she might have joined the organizing drive of the Congress of Industrial Organizations. While the felt injustice of married women working cannot be read as other than hostility, it takes on a different cast when seen from the perspective of work, rather than that of separate spheres. In the light of domesticity, it is a conservative plea for a return to traditional roles. In the light of workplace concerns, it becomes a demand for justice: for cooperation and sharing, and, arguably, for a different kind of market system. Articulated by both men and women, the injustice of wage work for those with alternate sources of incomes or for those without dependents was an idea that might have been conceived in, and sustained by, domesticity, but it took on a larger resonance in the prevailing climate of industrial distress. In practice, it was not gender neutral, and yet it reflects a conception of work-related roles that transcends a simple division into separate spheres.

What appears at first reading to be a defense of separate spheres and an affirmation of female domesticity contains a more complex statement about social reality. The letters articulate a vision of social order in which the provider role is related to both family and individual life cycle and in which men and women provide in different ways. They suggest a perception of jobs as a public resource to be disposed of fairly; and though there are clearly job hierarchies that are gender specific, the letters assume a pool of work that is available to be divided among the deserving. The definition of *deserving* rested primarily on the need to support oneself and others and only secondarily, in so far as the need was perceived as gender dependent, on sex. The letters reveal an inability or unwillingness to separate public and private values and an acknowledgment that dignity for both men and women lay in the preservation of both work possibilities and household order.

In challenging the moral authority of employers to hire who and where they please, they explicitly confront the neoclassical rationale that is said to organize the labor market and that demanded that the cheapest appropriate labor be sought and hired. Public opinion, gauged by this correspondence, insisted that this was wrong: letter writers repeatedly affirmed that the only appropriate criterion for hiring and firing was family need. While built-in assumptions about which sex most often had greater needs confirmed existing gender lines, gender difference did not add up to separate spheres. Rather, it seems to have constituted a coherent set of understandings from which to question the privileges of industrial power. We can speculate about the impact of these understandings on the introduction and shape of new social policies in the New Deal and on the beginning of the American welfare state. The exegesis in no way suggests abandoning the idea of domestic roles for women. It does encourage us to ask different kinds of questions. Among whom and under what conditions do gendered perceptions take the first place? What functions did gendered perceptions serve in particular times and places? Where did they impart a conservative outlook? Where did they lead to change?

But most important of all, in moving us from the dichotomous framework of separate spheres, a complex approach to gender as a part of everyone's world view enables us to interpret the past without the distortion of a single "difference" that becomes an overwhelming explanatory variable when the behavior of men and women is at issue. Gendered identity remains a critically important source of consciousness and behavior. As part of a historically contingent nexus that includes race, class, and ethnicity, it shapes the behavior of historical actors and frames the interpretations of historians. And, depending on its form, variety, and congruence in a particular historical setting, it can promote solidarity, consensus, disinterest, or conflict. But rarely in the same ways.

4. The Double Meaning of Equal Pay

The best interests of labor require the admission of women to full citizenship as a matter of justice to them and as a necessary step towards insuring and raising the scale of wages for all.

—American Federation of Labor resolution[1]

As the Equal Pay Bill came up for its final votes in the spring of 1963, the two sides squared off once again. The bill, which would prohibit differential wages for women doing "equal work on jobs the performance of which requires equal skill, effort and responsibility, and which are performed under similar working conditions," seemed destined to pass. Opponents, sensing defeat, sought to limit its scope and make it less intrusive. Advocates, fearing the opposition of business, compromised on key language and accepted an administrative apparatus that significantly narrowed the groups covered.[2] But the heart had gone out of the battle. Both sides understood what had only recently become apparent. As Congresswoman Katharine St. George, a New York State Republican and one of the bill's major supporters, put it, opposing equal pay "would be like being against motherhood." Norman Simler, staff member of the unenthusiastic President's Council of Economic Advisers and himself an opponent, counseled that fighting the bill was like "opposing virtue."[3] This then was the victorious anticlimax of the long struggle to acknowledge that women were entitled to what the Women's Bureau of the Department of Labor called the "rate for the job."

Eighteen years after the bill was first introduced into the House and more than half a century after women's and labor groups had adopted the fight for "equal pay for equal work"—a battle that rivaled in length that for suffrage itself—what had begun as an elusive quest became the law of the land. Hailed by the labor movement as "a landmark in the general movement on behalf of human rights,"[4] the new law was greeted sourly by business interests. "Millions of women will get pay raises over the next years," acknowledged one journal, "but countless others are in danger of losing their jobs."[5]

But what, in fact, had happened? How was it that a bill so hard fought could suddenly be classified as a victory for virtue and traditional American values? Was it, as business feared and activists in the Women's Bureau who had worked so hard for the bill hoped, a new milestone in the campaign for economic equality? Less than a year earlier, the *Wall Street Journal* had opened its report on the bill's progress with marked cynicism. "The little-noticed march of American womanhood toward perhaps its greatest conquest since winning the right to vote forty-two years ago is arousing belated pangs of agony among spokesmen for the nation's employers," ran a first page article.[6] How had the search for equal pay transformed itself from little more than wishful thinking to a milestone on the path to economic citizenship for women—the symbolic equivalent of motherhood and apple pie?

Some of the answers are to be found in the demographic shifts around the numbers and kinds of women drawn into wage work during the twentieth century. Some can be located in the economic effects of war and depression that altered perceptions of wage work and changed its meaning for men and women. But to fully understand the transformation requires an exploration of the changing meaning of the slogan itself. "Equal pay for equal work" is and has been deeply ambiguous. Its ambiguity captures mixed messages about gender and at the same time speaks to its shifting meanings over time. Thus, an exploration of the changing content of the phrase can help us to understand more than the relational nature of the wage. Because it speaks to perceptions of male and female relationships to work, it provides access to the subtle way gender is produced in the work force. As such, it offers us, as historians, a way of observing how gender is constructed.

Though some people trace the slogan back to the 1930s, it first became popular in the United States at the end of the nineteenth century. Then, women (frequently immigrants or rural migrants) were entering the labor force at an unprecedented rate, and innovative technology and managerial strategies encouraged experimentation with male and female workers. In a formal sense, its popularity paralleled its acceptance in Britain where the Trades Union Congress adopted the idea in 1888.[7] But even before that, it had appeared sporadically in trade union circles in the United States.[8] It emerged in 1898 as a recommendation of a congressional commission on industry, and popped up in repeated declarations of the American Federation of Labor until in 1915 the prestigious Commission on Industrial Relations proposed that "public opinion and legislation recognize that women should receive the same compensation as men for the same service."[9] Not until the United States entered World War I, however, did it seem to carry very much emotional resonance. Then, to protect the jobs of men who had been called to fight, the War Department, the Women in Industry Service, and the War Labor Board all supported the principle of equal pay in jobs "ordinarily performed by men"; and the War Labor Board regularly and consistently applied the principle in disputes that came before it.[10] In 1919 two states, Michigan and Montana, passed equal pay laws.

In the 1920s and after, equal pay became one of the few goals on which two opposing feminist groups could agree. The family-oriented Women's Bureau (of the Department of Labor) and the more individualistic feminists of the National Woman's Party joined in successfully supporting federal regulations that provided for equal pay in the civil service. And though they disagreed vehemently about the value of such protective labor legislation as the minimum wage for women only, they agreed that equal pay for equal work was a desirable goal.

What made this unnatural alliance possible was the double meaning contained in the slogan. Used by advocates of women's rights, equal pay was a rallying cry that confronted women's marginal status in the labor force. Its call for higher wages challenged the neoclassical paradigm that asserted that workers were paid according to the value of what they produced by pointing out that female workers were not paid by the same standards as men. It rejected the prevailing notion that women workers, unlike men, could be paid according to their needs, which were commonly assumed to be less than those of men. Instead, it embodied the demand for a wage appropriate to skill and independent of sex. It was also an expression of self-confidence and self-worth that belied the contemporary image of women workers as impermanent or unwilling to invest in their own training; and it offered a statement of female commitment to the labor force. It represented strength and individualism, sanctioning a definition of justice that treated women as individuals in their relationship to the work force.

But the slogan had another set of meanings as well. Used by the labor movement as well as by those who were family-oriented, it suggested exactly the opposite. It was a defensive reaction to the threat that employers might take advantage of the "cheap labor" of females to drive men out of the labor force. Thus, the slogan was filled with foreboding about women's capacity to upset traditional social roles. Uttered as a battle cry in the war to protect men's jobs, it could be read as the final defense of a sexually segregated work force: a fall-back position in the event that ideology, social pressure, and a tightly structured labor force failed to restrict women to their appropriate places. Under those circumstances, the insistence on equal pay could be counted on to discourage employers from hiring women. The phrase thus evoked traditional family roles and male prerogative at work and in the home. It reflected a sense of justice located in a defense of family lives and the male provider role.

The capacity of the phrase to reflect both individual aspiration and family norms accounts both for its appeal as a slogan and for its failure as a political goal. In practice, proponents could and frequently did argue simultaneously for both meanings. This was not hard to do in a social context that honored the family and conceived it as the medium of support for women and children. Equal pay appeared to sustain family well-being by seeming to protect male jobs. At the same time, it offered the promise of higher income, if not opportunity, to the relatively few women who passed through the barriers to opportunity it sustained.

Because the language and the defense of "equal pay for equal work" captured a shifting and diverse set of gendered expectations, the slogan served a variety of purposes—speaking to the individualistic and achievement-oriented aspirations of a minority of American women as it defended a socially sanctioned male privilege in the family and the labor force. As gendered expectations altered, and men and women began to see themselves as partners in the shared enterprise of self and family support, the meaning of the slogan changed as well, opening the door for a political effort that generated the support of a new generation of women. The slogan remained the same; the ambiguity within it shifted in ways that once again unified disparate groups around the interests of redefined gender expectations and encouraged them to see its goals as synonymous with American values. Thus, a look at the evolution of the rhetoric around equal pay for equal work tells us something about how the meanings and expectations of gender in relation to work finally translated into the politically successful struggle for the Equal Pay Act of 1963.

Until World War II, the vocabulary of most arguments for equal pay resisted the inclusion of individual rights. Framed by the Women's Bureau and its precursors within the Department of Labor, the issue resonated with concern for family values. The initial rhetoric can be extracted from one of the earliest rationales, written several months after the United States declared war on Germany in April 1917. Olga Halsey, a supervisor in the Women's Board of the Industrial Service Section of the Labor Department, sent her boss, Mary Van

Kleeck, an outline of arguments intended to persuade the War Labor Policies Board to support the principle of equal pay for equal work. Halsey offered three reasons for adopting the goal. The first was male fear of job competition. Male workers, she argued, would neither help nor support women who were undercutting their wages. If provoked by lower wages for women, they might resort to unionization or strike to exclude them altogether. The second was to attract women to jobs they might otherwise avoid—a strategy that would give employers a wider field of labor from which to choose and enhance their chances of hiring better workers. And, finally, there was the elusive matter of justice. "Women putting forth the same effort and producing the same results should have the same pay," Halsey argued. But the bold assertion of justice for women was immediately qualified by concern that, given the different interests of men and women in the workplace, justice for female wage earners not come at the expense of males. "It is hoped," she added protectively, "that much of the substitution may be only temporary; the places now filled by women should be returned to the men at men's present wages plus increases during the war period. If wages are cut or are maintained at their present level, regardless of the increased cost of living, as the result of employing women, it will be possible for the men to return only at a reduced wage."[11]

With many variations this set of arguments shaped the vortex around which swirled four decades of debate. Occupational segregation and the labor disruption that would attend its transgression, the need to maintain a competitive wage that respected tradition and yet did not close doors to women, and an apparently gender-neutral concept of justice—all these were at stake in "equal pay for equal work." Beneath the issues, at the heart of the debate, lay a persistent (though vulnerable) fealty to the capacity of a gender-segregated labor market to bring order to both home and work life. As long as this remained true, justice for women was perceived and constructed so as to acknowledge the prior claim of men to certain jobs and to a standard of wages from which women were excluded.

The evolving content of the early debate demonstrates its

close ties to the status quo. Fear of female competition with men dominated arguments for equal pay as they emerged among trade unionists in the early 1900s.[12] Because the argument incorporated a conception of males as family providers, it appeared to unify the interests of men and women, not divide them. Maintaining male wages in the face of competition from the cheap labor of women and protecting male jobs from the temptation to substitute cheaper female labor were not the selfish acts of one sex. They were the means of preserving traditional family life by enabling men to continue to provide for families. If, as the early twentieth century assumed, the male was still the provider, protection for men was synonymous with, not the opposite of, protection for women.

But the entry of large numbers of women into the labor force inevitably kept alive possibilities of justice based on women's individual rights and revealed the latent opposition between an appeal to women's family roles and their new places in the work force. In the single decade before 1900, the number of women earning wages increased by 66 percent.[13] Labeling women's competition "unfair," trade unions readily acknowledged what had become explicit and demanded equal pay. Union workers, intoned one *American Federationist* article, "know that woman has entered upon the industrial field to stay." Instead of protesting the inevitable, they should encourage women to organize "until they can secure the same wages as are paid to men for similar work performed."[14] The "cheap labor" of females was dangerous, argued suffragist Elizabeth Hauser. "When women organize and vote, they will get equal pay for equal work and they will no longer compete unfairly with men." Though fewer women would be employed, she continued, "this will not be a hardship because the increase in man's wages will give the family the larger income needed, without its being necessary for so many women to work outside the home."[15]

These themes were magnified during the first World War when women seemed to be moving rapidly into jobs previously the exclusive province of males. The quest for equal pay for equal work took on new intensity, but fear that women

might compete unfairly with men never completely elimi-
nated a subversive appeal for justice for women. Equal pay for
equal work would protect both men and women from wartime
exploitation, wrote Florence Thorne. "When women refuse to
work more cheaply than men, financial interests will not direct employers to substitute women for men but to choose
from among both men and women upon a basis of value of
service."[16]

Pressure from trade unionists, male and female, contributed to a general consensus that male rates needed to be
protected against the incursion of cheaper women. The U.S.
Bureau of Labor Statistics called for equal pay "as a matter of
public health." If women undercut "the standard wages of
men," they would reduce "the standards of living in the community," the Bureau argued, and thus threaten the public well-
being.[17] Mary Van Kleeck described equal pay "as the very
center of the present problem of labor in the war." Organized
men, she suggested, "have appeared unconscious of the influence of rates for women, who are their future competitors,
upon their own rates."[18] Summarizing the attitude of the National Women's Trade Union League, historian Elizabeth
Payne concurs. The league, she argues, feared "that men's
wages would fall as a result of women entering the marketplace." Underbidding men, thought Margaret Dreier
Robins, for many years its president, could only lead women to
"jeopardize their future home and potential motherhood."[19]

Given widely shared assumptions that, whatever else it
might do, equal pay for women would protect men's jobs, it
should not surprise us that as the slogan traveled through the
postwar decades it reinforced, rather than undermined, traditional sex roles. The Women's Bureau, a major force for keeping it alive, framed cogent reasons for preserving jobs for men
and explicitly defended the desirable consequences of preserving male privilege intact. Most men's jobs were not suitable for
women. If women took them, they owed it to their families and
to other women to protect the men to whom they rightfully
belonged by demanding equal wages.

At the core of this sensibility lay an inseparable connection between occupational segregation along gendered lines and the wage system. A woman's wage on men's jobs threatened to undermine occupational segregation by encouraging employers to substitute women for men. The equal wage promised to sustain it by removing employers' most tempting incentive to hire women. As the wage system helped to maintain a gender-segregated occupational structure, so a sexually segregated labor force maintained the integrity of the wage system by inhibiting comparisons of wages across gender lines. Such comparisons have historically rested on workers' perceptions of appropriate models against which they could judge whether their wages were fair and equitable.[20] For men those comparisons are said to reflect not only "the value of the job" but the relationship of jobs to each other. Equitable wages constitute one source of a worker's pride and dignity in his job. But women's wages have traditionally been justified in terms of the needs of the worker. They have assumed the bare cost of subsistence, not the value of the job, as the appropriate measure of a woman's worth. A gender-segregated labor force encouraged women to compare their wages to those of other women—a process that tended to limit aspirations for higher wages to what appeared possible.

Although equal pay seemed to be making a work-related demand, the rhetoric surrounding it was rooted in an understanding of social roles that assigned high wages and good jobs to the men who supported families. The slogan respected job segregation and limited wage comparisons by suggesting that segregated work could not and should not earn male pay. It supported the notion that comparing female to male pay was appropriate only for those women who were in fact performing the same jobs as men, and thus made it possible to retain one's self-respect at the lower wage typical of women's jobs. When occupational segregation broke down, even temporarily, as it did, for example, during World War I, inevitable wage tensions resulted. The Women in Industry Service noted that women who had formerly been satisfied with much lower wages protested when they discovered they earned less than men doing the same jobs. The service recorded the "discontent and ill

feeling . . . which resulted in careless work" that was characteristic of women with "good habits of work" who were taken
on at twenty cents an hour only to discover that "young boys
with no training at all" were hired in at thirty-one cents an
hour.[21] As long as it was sustained by occupational segregation, equal pay for equal work restricted comparisons between
men and women workers by implying that those who did not
work alongside men could not expect to compare themselves
to them.

In the face of the closely knit understanding of gendered
jobs and wages, any efforts by the Women's Bureau to act on
the image of individual rights implicit in the call for equal pay
for equal work fell by the wayside. During the 1930s, for example, the Women's Bureau simultaneously urged "a rate for the
job" and supported minimum wage laws that covered only
women. The first position assumed a wage paid for the value of
the work performed. The second rested on an assessment of
women's needs—a position that was justified by the sex of the
worker. These seemingly contradictory positions can be reconciled only if we accept that to the women who staffed the
bureau as to many female activists, the wage was understood
as provision for a family, rather than as the reward of achievement on the job. It thus led the Women's Bureau to accept a
language that referred freely to "men's jobs." The reality of a
gender-divided work force reduced the contradiction from a
practical reality to a theoretical possibility. Since occupational segregation in practice vitiated comparisons across gender lines, the minimum wage offered a practical alternative to
those consigned by the division of labor to low-paying jobs by
offering them some protection. At the same time, the fight for
equal pay permitted comparisons of wages in the relatively
few jobs held by men and women.

If the practical meaning of equal pay for equal work was
diffused by its respect for gender segregation in jobs, the family orientation that was its focal point never went entirely
uncontested. Agents of the Women's Bureau euphemistically
but not inaccurately referred to the alternative meaning posed
by the slogan as "educational." Stifled but never wholly elimi-

nated by the equal pay slogan, the message of a potential independence offered sporadic encouragement to violate traditional sex roles and to seek monetary rewards. Samuel Gompers, head of the American Federation of Labor, recognized the phenomenon: "Women who by their own labor earn wages sufficient to support them independently have the power to choose and direct their own lives. They are free from the galling dependence and deference that invariably accompany a condition of either total or partial dependence upon others for the necessities of life."[22] The consequences of such independence could not be measured. Equal pay, claimed a stalwart female unionist, could be described as "in furtherance of the highest ideals of womanhood. It expresses self-respect, conscious of ability to render service, jealously guarding dignity against undervaluation in the eyes of others."[23] The labor movement called on these definitions in the 1930s to sustain support for equal pay under the seniority provisions in its newly negotiated collective bargaining contracts. Not to include women and people of color in these provisions would violate the principle of job entitlement that lay at the heart of seniority systems. To include these groups, however, was to acknowledge their individual rights to jobs without regard to their location in the family or to family need—a particular problem in view of the general attitude of many male workers to women.[24] Caught in a bind, trade union leaders found themselves defending equal pay on the principle of every worker's right to a job while their members took the opposite position. One South Bend, Indiana, auto body worker suggested that employers should be made to "pay the same wages that they pay for men, and they would not have any women working on the job."[25]

Similarly, the argument from individual rights continued to inform the National Women's Party's efforts to achieve equal pay. In the worst years of the depression, it urged General Hugh Johnson, head of the National Recovery Administration, to adopt "a general policy for the NRA which will give women an equal opportunity for self-support."[26] In the same period, the Women's Bureau sought the same end, "a rate for the job," and persuaded the NRA to include equal pay provisions in three-quarters of its industrial codes on the grounds that they would reduce employer incentive to substitute women for men.[27] These exceptions notwithstanding, the argument for equal pay remained firmly rooted in the needs of family life.

The subverted or hidden argument emerged during and immediately after the second World War when the drive for equal pay joined forces with a powerful new sense of rectitude. Its stimulus came from three sources: a breakdown of occupational segregation during the war years; a new ideology of consumerism and prosperity rooted in the experience of depression and in popular interpretations of Keynesian economics that legitimated women's desire for income; and a political climate that connected higher standards of living to America's place in the world. These developments encouraged a new emphasis on individual rights consistent with the long-suppressed meaning of equal pay.

Students of the second World War have frequently pointed out that employers and male workers strove to limit occupational mobility for women.[28] While this is undoubtedly the case, still enough temporary replacements were made to create new opportunities for comparing male and female wages. To women workers, many of them veterans of the work force, new only to men's jobs, the wartime situation exposed long-buried arguments for individual rights to fairness and justice. From the grass roots, it seemed, women rejected the notion that male needs constituted a compelling reason for higher pay and simultaneously asserted the validity of women's demands. "In our system," complained a Racine, Wisconsin, schoolteacher to Bertha Nienburg, associate director of the Women's Bureau, "single men receive two hundred dollars more annually than the women and married men receive five hundred more."[29] And a cleaning lady making thirty-four and one-half cents an hour fumed, "The men janitors here doing the same work without the matron responsibilities are receiving 62 and 72 [cents] per hour."[30] Nor were direct comparisons lacking. A female welder protested to Frances Perkins that the women in her plant had to "put up a scrap" for every wage increase they had received: I started that, she said, "because I learned that a man welder sitting across from me was getting 90c. per hour." He, she noted, was "an inexperienced welder just starting on production." The women welders were then brought up to the male level, but at the time of their next scheduled increase, they were turned down "even tho we are more experienced, and are putting out more production. More in fact than the men who formerly held the job at a higher rate of pay." She "had been working for a number of months and was earning 80c. per hour."[31]

As wartime conditions allowed women to breach time-honored barriers to occupational segregation, the gendered content of the wage relation began to undergo clear, if inconsistent, changes. A Dayton, Ohio, Frigidaire worker wrote FDR that she would try to explain why she believed the women in her plant ought to have equal pay. "The men and women's jobs are nearly identical," she wrote. "We girls can hold down any job that a man can we have done, most of them are doing it now [sic]."[32] This recognition encouraged a broader set of comparisons, which seem to have been closely related to a redefinition of female needs and to an effort to redefine an appropriate wage. Nora Galloway, a South Bend, Indiana, widow with two children to support who worked as a tool checker, wrote to FDR "to find out what you think of all these women working in defence plants doing mens work and only receiving childrens pay." Citing her family responsibilities, she suggested that she was angry enough to switch jobs for more pay. "I think I should have the same money an hour as Studebakers factory pays or I going to quit where I am and go to Studebakers where they pay women 70c an hour to start and after your there a while you get $1.05 an hour." Lest she be accused of being unpatriotic, she quickly added a second reason for moving. At her present wage, she wrote, she could not buy enough defense bonds; if she went where she "could get more money and buy more bonds," not only would this contribute to the war effort, but she would "have something when the war is over. I am," she concluded with a burst of passion, "just as good to have it as any one. . . . Their men make as much as $15.00 a day in two days these men get more than I get for 6 days and I have a family to support and rent to pay."[33]

The pressure for justice required a rationale that contradicted those prevalent in earlier notions of equal pay. Women claimed that female needs were not different from those of men in any way that mattered. "I for one have been wondering for some time why a woman's salary in most all cases are so much lower than men," wrote Ethel Lee of Covington, Kentucky, to Mary Anderson. In an argument that prefigured one of the important issues of the postwar debate, she noted, "for entertainment, eats, rent, there is no difference . . . the divorce cases are rising all the time. Who can depend on a man for support?"[34]

Implicit in these letters are the dangers of breaking down occupational segregation. They open the possibility of comparisons with male workers that had previously been out of the realm of possibility. But more importantly, these comparisons threaten the meaning of justice that is located in custom and tradition and the image of the male as provider. As women discovered that their experience negated old rationalizations for protecting male workers, they looked toward a new definition of fairness to their families and to themselves. In the war years the rhetoric that supported differential pay scales began to seem increasingly absurd. The employer who told the Women's Bureau interviewer, "Let's face it. . . . we hire women because they are cheaper," was only articulating free market principles, but to the interviewer his answer seemed patently unjust. In the wake of depression and war, the discrepancy between the notion that the lesser financial responsibilities of women justified pay differentials and the tremendous demands for support on most wage-earning women could no longer be sustained. "Needs-based" arguments became the subject of ridicule.

At the same time, economic analysts noted that the new comparisons posed a problem. Equalizing pay rates for male and female factory workers doing the same or comparable jobs raised the wages of some women and thus violated what was

euphemistically called the "custom of the industry" or traditional notions of wage differentials between men and women.
Since these rates reflected women's social roles and incorporated gendered meanings, altering them would inevitably dis-
turb the equilibrium that tied wages to prevailing understandings of gender relations.

Several strategies emerged to combat this danger. As it
stepped up pressure for equal pay, the Women's Bureau continued to argue for saving men's jobs for the long term. Mary
Anderson described her own experiences at juggling the issues
this way: To convince union men that equal pay was in their
own interests, she wrote,

I appealed to their selfishness in terms of preserving their own jobs.
. . . I said, "You in the union are now very strong; you have a tremendous membership; you have lots of money from dues; you can do now
what you can't do later when the war is over and jobs become scarce;
. . . There will be competition for jobs; then the employer will hire the
cheapest workers, and while I am interested in women getting work
because they have to live just as much as anybody else, at the same
time I am not interested in women being exploited and used to lower
the standard of living." I then said you can forestall that now if you get
into your union contracts the principle of the same wages for women
as for men.[35]

The War Labor Policies Board tried to combat the diseq-
uilibrium by permitting but not insisting on raises for women
doing the same or "comparable" jobs as men while adamantly
refusing to consider wage raises for women who worked in jobs
that historically paid less than those of men. Thus, the board's
General Order no. 16 permitted, but did not require, employers
to "equalize the wage or salary rates paid to females with the
rates paid to males for comparable quality and quantity of
work on the same or similar operations." At the same time, it
contended that the rates of women in job classifications "to
which only women have been assigned in the past . . . are
presumed to be correct."[36]

Some employers abetted this effort by trying to keep rates
for women deliberately lower than those of men. One person-

nel manager explained that in order to keep the rates of female factory workers "somewhat in line with other women's rates," his company set women's starting rates five cents per hour lower than those of men.[37] A radio manufacturing company wanted the same differential in order "to maintain a dual wage structure on the grounds of traditional differences which had always existed between men's and women's rates."[38] When such rates were challenged by male workers for undermining the male wage scale and by women for reasons of fairness, they released a flood of complaints that encouraged comparisons among wage rates in general.

The potential danger in all of these defenses against increasing women's pay in women's jobs lay in the questions they raised about the justice of differential pay for any job that had been assigned according to sex. "Any equalizing of rates of pay for women on factory jobs," noted one economic analyst, "has to be considered in relation to the office." Some companies, he suggested, should "consider the ultimate establishment of a single series of rate ranges for both factory and office jobs, with the same starting rates in both cases—one scale that is universal for men or women, shop or office, grade for grade." Failure to confront the issue of differential rates squarely, he warned, would have dire results. "Necessity will compel the white collar workers to turn to outside agencies for the consideration they deserve."[39]

This argument, then referred to as *equitable pay*, we would now call *comparable worth*. A University of Michigan economist summed up the difference this way: "The slogans 'equal pay for equal work' and 'the rate for the job' both express too narrowly the real objective of equality of economic opportunity between the sexes, for they concentrate attention too exclusively on the rather few occupations which are common to both sexes in peacetime, or in which women replace men during wartime." He proposed a program of job evaluation that would attempt "to make proper allowance for all compensable factors, to the end that wage rates shall be equitable, not merely within but as between all occupations."[40]

In July 1945 the Women's Bureau decided to explore this

position. A consequence of an evolving shift in its equal pay
rationale, the choice reflected its efforts to develop a "long-
term program of full employment opportunity" and to make a
case for "a rate of wages corresponding to the actual value of
the job . . . or the process . . . perform[ed] in the industry." The
equal pay principle, the memo argued, had two parts. It required "the payment to women of the same rate as men where
they are employed on processes that are the same, or substan-
tially comparable," to those currently or previously employing men. "*But more than this*," bureau officials emphasized, "it
necessitates a review of rates in jobs that ordinarily are or
customarily have been performed by women." Here was an
effort not to move women into men's jobs but to sever the
connection between wage and gender segregation in the job
market. The memo insisted on the need for "consistent technical appraisals of the actual value of specific jobs done by
workers." The absence of such efforts, it indicated, in language
that previewed that of the 1980s, "has led to the payment of
women at rates below those fixed for male common labor even
in operations that involve a considerable degree of skill, dexterity, speed and care. In such a situation, there can be no
question that women are being paid a substandard wage in
relation to their performance and their value to the industry
just as surely as when the wage paid them is less than their
living costs." Until recently, the memo noted, correcting these
inequities "involved chiefly a matter of justice to a body of
workers paid less than the rate to which the job entitles them."
But now, it added, drawing on rationales that came from the
Keynesian revolution, "it is an essential part" of the country's
objective "of securing a high level of employment and increasingly high standards of living for the whole people."[41]

The Women's Bureau was apparently serious in its efforts to
explore the possibility of eliminating the weight of "custom
and tradition" in setting women's wages. Anderson herself
commented shortly after the war that the slogan "equal pay for
equal work" was misleading. "What women workers really
want is "the rate for the job" regardless of sex. In many instances women's work is just as skilled as men's even though

not equal or identical with men's." Thus, she continued, she supported the wording of the bill currently before Congress that prohibited any employer from paying differential wages to men and women doing "work of comparable quality and quantity."[42] Though ambiguous about how far she would be willing to take the comparable work principle, Anderson supported efforts of the bureau to explore the limits of equal pay by conducting a series of investigations and hearings on industrial wage-determination studies in 1946 and 1947. Partly in response to the War Labor Board's demand for some rationale for raising wages during the war, such studies had proliferated. Their aim was to assess the relative quantities of skill, effort, and responsibility located in particular jobs and then compare them with each other. The Women's Bureau, seeking an objective measure of what women's jobs were worth, now attempted to assess their impact by reviewing the studies of dozens of employers. Their conclusions, which appear not to have been published in bulletin form, were mixed.

While theoretically, evaluation of job content ought to lead to pay scales that removed the sex of the worker as a factor and therefore to an increase in women's rates, in practice eliminating gender proved more difficult. Because the ratings involved a level of subjective judgment about the value of job content, the ratings themselves reflected the biases of those who developed them; and therefore, gender bias was built into ratings systems. Frequently, evaluation schemes and point weights were adopted by management alone; but even when unions participated, there was little guarantee that the weights would be gender neutral. Typically, work that required speed, dexterity, and the ability to tolerate boredom weighed less than heavy, dirty, and outside tasks. A Chicago mail-order house defended its rate differentials by arguing that "men's work is generally heavier and also that men can usually get and expect to get higher rates." Like the company, union representatives saw little wrong with this argument. In this case, "a differential was thought justified because generally the men's work is more demanding physically and also the family and social responsibilities of men" needed to be taken into account."[43]

A second factor influencing rating systems was that, in deference to custom, tradition, and the market, employers continued to insist on separate pay schedules for men and women and particularly on separate scales for progression and merit raises. The Singer Manufacturing Company proposed "a bi-lateral wage line maintaining the historic differentials between men's and women's jobs."[44] The Dowst Manufacturing Company in Chicago offered women a flat rate of sixty cents an hour that did not increase no matter how competent the worker became. Men, in contrast, could earn merit increases that raised their pay from a starting rate of seventy-five cents to ninety cents an hour.[45] Finally, even where a rating system seemed fair on its face, employers relied on sex segregation to maintain wage differentials. Repeatedly, the Women's Bureau noted that the issue of comparable wages never emerged because women were simply not employed in many jobs.

But in the end it was not these internal problems that scuttled the incipient campaign for comparable worth. Rather, it was that equal pay, unlike comparable worth, sustained a major thrust of the postwar economy—to increase consumption by enhancing productivity. The nation had emerged from the Great Depression and the war committed to Keynesian principles of economic growth as the key to national well-being. Higher standards of living could, it was widely thought, be attained by a self-reinforcing cycle of enhanced productivity and incentives to consume. These precepts demanded the participation of women as workers and as consumers.

Equal pay supported these goals in two ways: it encouraged women to earn wages that would contribute to higher standards of living; yet it promised to reduce friction in the workplace by maintaining the occupational segregation that would continue the traditional relation between male and female wages. As the Women's Bureau itself pointed out, "If equal pay is required for the same work, then it follows that differentials in pay are justified because of differences in job content. Such wage differences—under the equal pay principle—are equitable, morally justified, and, under equal pay law, may acquire legal sanction."[46] That raised the question of the extent to which job content should determine wages. In a period when rapid technological change threatened to deskill some jobs, making them available to women, the notion of equal pay protected the fiction that certain jobs were "men's jobs" and required greater rewards. Accepting equal pay for the relatively few jobs in which men and women were employed implicitly placed the Women's Bureau sanction of differential pay on those in which only women worked. But it confronted the Women's Bureau with several hard questions: "Is there any danger that the lower differentials established for women workers which receive the sanction of law will have long run adverse effects on women's rates? Will precedents be more firmly established which will be difficult to cope with?" And would such precedents ultimately benefit "the employer who maintained lower differentials for women?"[47] Equal pay protected the family and the high level of consumption, guaranteed by high male wages. Its cost was occupational segregation and female inequality.

Job content analysis, on the other hand, assumed a wage structure independent of the sex of the worker. It offered to overcome traditional or customary wage rates that were rooted in prejudices about male and female sex roles but made no claims to tie the structure of wages to notions of male family responsibility. Indeed, it was widely seen as a "bloodless" way of reducing rates on the basis of reduced skills. Gender justice thus seemed to negate the possibility of an appropriate family standard of living. Reluctantly, Women's Bureau analysts came to the position that there might well be "a conflict between the application of the job content principle and the broader social philosophy of the living wage." What, they asked, would be the ultimate consequence for women of a policy in which "maintaining as high a standard of living as the economy can afford seems to be the immediate and long run objective?"[48]

As the argument played itself out, it looked as if only a sacrifice of gender equality could maintain the high wages necessary for continuing prosperity. It could be understood as in the national self-interest. It was easy to sell. Yet the sacrifice does not seem to have been easily made. Frieda Miller, then director of the Women's Bureau, began her testimony for the 1945 bill with a short prelude. "It is common knowledge," she said, "that wage rates have always been lower in the major woman-employing industries, such as textiles, retail trade, laundries, and other service industries. I pass over these without comment."[49]

The bill introduced by Claude Pepper and Wayne Morse at the urging of the Women's Bureau in 1945 reflected these changes. Its preamble argued that inequitable compensation based on sex was an unfair wage practice that could lead to labor disputes; depress "wages and living standards of employees, male and female"; interfere with and prevent "the maintenance of an adequate standard of living" among workers and their families, especially on the families of "deceased or disabled veterans"; prevent the maximum utilization "of our available labor resources and plant capacity essential for full production, in war and peace"; and endanger the national security and the general welfare. The new rhetoric around equal pay did not abandon the notion that women competed with men for jobs and wages, so much as it subsumed issues of wages and job competition into national well-being, and altered the character of the argument.

In support of this rationale, the Women's Bureau pulled out the stops in its efforts to get an equal pay bill passed. It created a National Equal Pay Commission headed by Mary Anderson. Under cover of the commission, the bureau planned a media campaign to publicize the movement for equal pay. It sent out upwards of sixty letters to popular magazines, to the house organs of major women's groups, and to labor union papers, offering them articles on equal pay or material they could use to write their own.[50] A handful of popular magazines accepted the offer, and a sturdy two dozen union journals agreed to run articles. The bureau pressed Congress for action on equal pay and managed to get hearings in 1945, 1948, and 1950. This effort was followed in 1952 by a National Conference on Equal

Pay, out of which grew a new National Committee on Equal
Pay.

Clearly, equal pay was on the agenda in a way it had never
been. Beginning in 1943, one state after another passed equal
pay laws. First Washington in 1943, then Illinois and New York
in 1944. Massachusetts, Rhode Island, New Hampshire, and
Pennsylvania followed in successive years. By the end of 1955,
sixteen states and Alaska had equal pay laws on the books.[51]
Both major party platforms supported equal pay in 1948 and
sporadically thereafter. Between 1945 and 1950, equal pay
bills were introduced and hearings held in every session of
Congress. In the 1950s none of the seventy-two bills introduced
into Congress got a hearing. Still, the issue did not subside.
President Eisenhower included support of an equal pay act in
his state of the union address in 1956. Trade unions continued
to include equal pay provisions in their collective bargaining
agreements.[52] More than a decade of discussion and exploration preceded the final push for passage in 1962.[53]

The political appeal of arguments for equal pay that rested
on continuing economic growth derived a larger justification
from the new place of the United States in the world. High
standards of living would help to justify America's claim to
world leadership and legitimize its fight against communism.
The context helped to link the individual rights piece of the
equal pay argument to the Keynesian revolution. The link
emerged during the war years. Women who were discrimi-
nated against in the labor force "cannot be expected to exhibit
the necessary morale" to sustain high levels of production,
suggested one rationale. And, as if in afterthought, "It is also
important to the morale of men on the job as well as those
leaving for military duty to be confident that existing wage
structures will not be undermined in their absence."[54] These
references to the morale of producers merged into incentives
to pull increasing numbers of women into the labor force. Even
employers who preferred to pay women less in deference to
custom conceded that the elimination of wage differentials
were "an important factor in getting more women into the
labor market."[55] In the postwar years, the continuing de-

mands of production increasingly pulled women into the labor force. The argument that women's morale as producers required equal pay merged into the effort to deploy human resources in effective support of the national goal of prosperity. Equal pay became a positive force for the high productivity of workers, male and female, and one engine of a consumer-driven economy.

The transformation required renegotiating the meaning of the wage. The living wage and the minimum wage for women had incorporated sharply differentiated conceptions of the needs of male and female workers. The living wage called up images of wage-earning men who were married and supported families. It assumed dependent women to whom the obligation to prevent starvation was merely a byproduct. In the competition for jobs and wages, the male's historic prerogatives were sustained by the moral claims of the family. The minimum wage can, in some sense, be said to have been designed to pick up the residual women without families. It rested on definitions of women's needs, apart from family, and conceptions that women were entitled only to what they "absolutely required" for health and decency. In sharp contrast, the postwar articulation of equal wages rested on a conception of consumption that, though directly benefiting an individual family, benefited the nation's families and ultimately, by increasing national well-being, strengthened democracy. "Conscious efforts to employ human and economic resources fully would result in a higher national standard of living," one Women's Bureau memo noted.[56] Drawing on the lessons of the depression, analysts agreed that if women were paid more they would spend more. "Equal pay will tend to increase effective consumer demand, thus aiding efforts to achieve full employment."[57] The new idiom removed the discussion of equal pay from the self-interest of the job holder to the realm of family well-being. It assumed that women, like men, were family providers, and sought equal pay in order to incorporate women into a shared struggle for the survival of democracy. The language of citizenship had become the sanction of equal pay. "There perhaps was a time in the country's history when a man, because of his commanding position as the head of the family and breadwinner, was entitled to more compensation than the single woman," said the bill's Senate sponsor, Pat McNamara. "But in modern-day America, women's role as a provider, for not only herself but her family, has become an essential role."[58] To this rationale George Addes, international secretary-treasurer of the UAW-CIO, added the clincher. Equal pay for equal work, he noted, was "one of the equal rights in the promise of American democracy regardless of color, race, sex, religion or national origin."[59] Equal pay had shed its oppositional content to appear instead in a patriotic garb.

The message formulated in the early postwar years remained consistent throughout the period. Equal pay was a matter of simple justice, and it was in the national interest to implement it. It drew on expanded notions of American democracy encouraged first by the war itself and then by the cold war. And it integrated the economic lessons of the depression and expectations for high standards of living with myths of American homogeneity and strength in the face of the cold war. Images of ambitious women disappeared, as did threats to occupational segregation. Instead, a combination of moral suasion and economic self-interest held the day.

But the core argument, echoed and reechoed by witnesses for the bill, derived from efforts to redefine justice for women as a function of their individual rights rather than of family responsibilities, while suppressing the notion that individual rights could open the door to ambition. In the prewar language of equal pay, women had been creatures of the family for whom equal pay implied an antimale provider and therefore antifamily stance. To protect male jobs required suppressing whatever elements of individual self-realization existed in equal pay, in favor of loyalty to the family. But the twin experiences of depression and war, which placed the individual efforts of women in the service of families, altered this perspective. Equal pay now meant the capacity to help the family and the nation. The implicit possibility of achieving personal goals was suppressed. The core of the new sense of justice was a powerful conflation of individual rights, family responsibilities, and consumer needs that enabled the idea of equal pay to overcome free market principles.

Testimony for equal pay repeated through several sets of hearings drew on notions of fairness and justice that had entered into the dialogue during the war. The hearings for the 1945 bill located them in women's wartime contributions, which, according to Secretary of Labor Lewis Schwellenbach, amply supported the case for justice. The proposed legislation was desirable "as a matter of fairness."[60] The preamble to the bill noted that the disabilities and deaths of veterans left many wives and widows vulnerable. At the 1948 hearings the notion of simple justice was echoed so frequently as to appear self-evident and to need no defense. Elizabeth Christman, testifying for the Women's Trade Union League, insisted that "equal pay is a matter of simple justice."[61] A union representative suggested that equal pay was "a matter of simple justice to the women of our country."[62] Joseph Beirne, president of the Communications Workers of America, echoed the sentiment. The women pressing for equal pay were not "attempting to achieve some vague or lofty ideal," he testified. Rather, they were seeking a "simple principle of fundamental justice."[63] From that point on, the cloak of justice masked the retreat from the marketplace that the principle of equal pay reflected.

Frieda Miller, then head of the Women's Bureau, began her testimony with an eloquent plea to the subcommittee to reject notions that either men or women were paid on the basis of their needs. "A differential wage rate paid workers in accordance with the size of their families," she noted, had been rejected by economists because it "undermines the accepted principle of 'the rate for the job' and would provide an incentive for employers to engage unmarried workers in preference to those with families."[64] Others were more explicit. "The principle of a 'family wage' has never become established in this country as a basis for compensation. A single man is paid as much as a married man for doing the same job. Pay is for work done, rather than for the number of dependents of the worker," testified Secretary of Labor Schwellenbach.[65] No sex differential applied, suggested other witnesses, "when women spend the money they earn. Grocery stores do not have double standard price tags, one for men customers, one for women. A loaf of bread is just a loaf of bread and sells for so much. It makes no difference whether a woman pays for it or a man. . . . There are no male or female tax rates."[66] As one female union member put it, "It is only a matter of simple justice that we ask for. We are entitled to the price for the work which we do."[67] If equal pay was for work done, then it followed that equal pay was neither more nor less than fair pay. "The principle of 'equal pay for equal work,'" said Maurice Tobin in his first annual report as secretary of labor, "is as basic to the American way of life as are the guarantees of free speech, free thought, free press, free assembly, and free association."[68]

By the time the Women's Bureau convened its National Conference on Equal Pay in 1952, failure to participate in the rhetoric of justice had become a matter for rebuke. Secretary of Labor Tobin castigated differential pay as "a practice neither fair nor logical. It arises from a state of mind, a bad business habit, a cultural pattern that will ultimately be eradicated."[69] This moral stance characterized the struggle up to the end. In 1963 Senator Pat McNamara, chairman of the Senate Committee on Labor and Public Welfare, berated those who shared the "ancient but outmoded belief that a man, because of his role in society, should be paid more than a woman even though his duties are the same."[70]

The capstone was that everyone, except perhaps for some unscrupulous employers, could be expected to benefit from a law that rejected outmoded beliefs and insisted on justice. Equal pay, argued Frieda Miller and others, "will promote the general welfare by protecting wage levels and thereby sustain consumer purchasing power and family living standards."[71] Having learned the lessons of the depression well, advocates of equal pay applied them diligently to their cause. "Should women's wages for comparable work be less than men's," argued the League of Women Shoppers, drawing on an old argument, "it is inevitable that women as a cheaper labor market will be used to replace men or that men's wages will be reduced to the women's level." But then came the punch line: "The downward spiral commences with reduced purchasing power for the consumer, decreased production and employment."[72] As the AFL put it, "To pay women less than men is to tear down the American standard of life."[73]

By contrast, wage discrimination was positively un-American. It would result, argued Frieda Miller, in "lower levels of earnings for all" and end ultimately in "reduced purchasing power and standards of living." But Miller continued with a forceful warning: "In consideration of our national objective of high living standards and full employment, I submit that we cannot afford to risk the threat to general wage levels that unequal pay to women involves."[74] Lewis Schwellenbach agreed that "low wage standards decrease the national purchasing power" while equal pay would serve to "counteract influences that depress wage levels."[75] His successor, Maurice Tobin, used harsher language. "Undercutting the wage scale by one or another group in society jeopardizes that most desirable of all social goals—an adequate standard of living for the family. Equal pay is essential to a healthy economy."[76]

Unequal pay would not only depress standards of living; it would, it was thought, contribute to a host of other evils in the labor force. It would, for example, prevent the maximum utilization of the labor supply by discouraging employment and inhibiting labor mobility. Schwellenbach put it this way: "Sex differentials in wage rates are a serious brake upon the best use of our labor resources and to that extent inhibit full production." Discriminatory wages, he suggested, created a "frozen labor market" from which industry would suffer because workers would be unable to move freely from job to job as situations demanded.[77] In February 1963 John Kennedy's secretary of labor, Willard Wirtz, made the same argument. Transmitting the bill to Lyndon Baines Johnson, then president of the Senate, he argued that "among other compelling reasons for its enactment is the necessity to utilize fully the skills of women in our labor force."[78] Moreover, sex differentials would produce resentment among women workers. Recalling the wartime experience, Senator Wayne Morse com-

mented on how "in the early stages of the war, failure to pay
equal wages for equal work resulted in a great deal of labor
unrest."[79] The comment was echoed by Senator Pat
McNamara of Michigan in 1963 who feared the effect of poor
morale among workers who were not fairly paid.[80]

Under these circumstances adopting equal pay, as the Conference on Equal Pay concluded in 1952, would yield "better
personnel relationships and practices." It was simply a "good
business principle."[81] Failing to adopt it, as Senator McNamara put it in the 1963 debates, "not only creates a severe
hardship for the non-discriminating employer," but, as Representative Ralph Rivers concurred, contributes to the "process
of allowing unscrupulous employers to gain a competitive
advantage."[82] These arguments echoed those of Senator Morse
nearly twenty years earlier. Differential rates might be to the
short-term competitive advantages of some employers, he had
said then, but the plea for competitive rates ought not to
permit them to "hold on to discriminatory practices."[83]

Into these arguments proponents integrated the rhetoric of
the cold war. An undercurrent of the campaign in the 1950s
was the degree to which more efficient production would help
fight communism by encouraging preparedness. The Women's
Bureau's choice of Arthur Fleming to keynote its 1952 conference on equal pay could not have been an accident. Fleming
was then the Labor Department's manpower chief in the Office
of Defense Mobilization. He rose to the occasion. "Whenever
we refuse to put into operation this concept of equal pay for
equal work," he argued, "we are just refusing to face the manpower aspects of our defense mobilization program in an intel-
ligent and realistic manner."[84] Fleming, who became
Eisenhower's secretary of health, education, and welfare and
then a contributing editor of *Good Housekeeping*, continued
the argument into the 1960s. Women who participated in "the
crusade for militant programs" such as equal pay, he concluded a 1962 *Good Housekeeping* article, would "have the
satisfaction of knowing they are helping to make available to
the nation human resources that will be desperately needed in
the challenging years to come."[85] Claude Pepper, veteran of

many equal pay battles, supported the 1963 Equal Pay Act
with a stereotypical cold war warning: "Khrushchev has pre-
dicted that by 1970, Russia will overtake this country economically. We need all the incentive that we can provide to the
labor force of this Nation to keep America superior in economic power and progress in the free world today."[86]

Questions of national image vied with those of production
for victory in the cold war battle. Higher standards of living
would illustrate the superiority of the American economic
system to that of the communist world. The issue merged as
early as 1945 and persisted. "Today when tolerance and justice
are so needed to help set the world on the road to peace we in
the United States who must take the lead in winning peace for
all time, cannot afford to permit discrimination."[87] In a dramatic escalation of rhetoric that matched the escalation of the
cold war itself, proponents of the 1963 act insisted that "the
principle of equal pay . . . is fundamental to the American free
enterprise system."[88] As he brought the bill to the floor of the
House, Representative Adam Clayton Powell, chairman of the
House Committee on Education and Labor, participated in the
flourish: "The payment of wages on a basis other than that of
the job performed is not only harmful to the individual worker
and our economy, but also to our Nation's image abroad."[89]

In short, proponents of equal pay adopted a rhetoric that fit
the mood of the period. "Fighting for those rights," as one
union journal summed up the struggle, "was the democratic
thing to do. It also is the smart thing to do—smart for male
workers, who will be protecting their own wage level; smart
for employers who will be protecting themselves against unfair tactics of competitors who try to produce cheap products
with cheap labor; and smart for consumers who will be protecting themselves and the economy from unscrupulous
schemers who have no regard for quality of products."[90]

Against the weight of such patriotic rhetoric, employers and
economists who fell back on old arguments could not prevail.
Women, went the old arguments, deserved to be paid less
because they invested less in the labor market. Their attachment to the home and their responsibilities for families justi-

fied a lower wage. Women, claimed business representatives, simply cost more to employ. They were not opposed to equal pay in principle, argued business representatives, but legislators needed to take account of the additional costs of women as workers. According to employers, these costs included women's more frequent absenteeism, their high turnover, the longer training period required to prepare them for jobs, and the closer levels of supervision required.[91] They also included the costs of such state-mandated amenities as minimal numbers of toilets, appropriate lunchrooms, and regulations governing shorter hours and rest periods.

Opponents argued that paying women equally would force employers to give up the possibility of investing in male permanency.[92] The argument revealed something of the social expectations that constituted part of the hidden content of the male wage. Men, but not women, were worth cultivating for something called versatility or their future benefit to the company. While the principle of equal pay embodied a rate of wages corresponding to actual performance, personnel directors frankly declared that a man "may be paid more because the company is training him for a responsible position and wants to be sure to keep him with the company either until training is completed or the position opens.[93] The Equal Pay Bill, which would prohibit companies from paying men extra during a holding period, threatened to deprive industry of this valuable source of labor. As a result, commented one company president, young men who had been hired as secretaries might lose that option. We always knew, he commented, "that there was a possible potential of their rising to more important jobs, supervising a large number of men. If this law is passed, we will hire women for all secretarial positions and be deprived of this avenue of advancement."[94]

Such costs could be concretely measured, suggested business representatives. One witness estimated the additional costs of female workers at anywhere from twenty-one to thirty cents an hour. The number was compiled by calculating the price of amenities that women required. The cost of extra female facilities, one manufacturer estimated, was one-tenth of a cent per hour. Extra rest periods came to ten cents per hour.[95] These costs, argued Senator Paul Findley who championed the cause, were attributable to "the indisputable fact that women are more prone to homemaking and motherhood than men." But Findley failed to persuade other legislators to amend the bill to allow employers to take those costs into account, because otherwise "employers will tend to cut back on female employment."[96]

These arguments, which expressed covert beliefs that women's home roles still took precedence over their work lives, could not overcome the powerful ideology of justice for individual American citizens. By the mid 1950s ultimate passage seemed certain. As Secretary of Labor Maurice Tobin commented at the 1952 Equal Pay Conference, "Ask the average businessman, the laboring man, and the public servant whether he believes in equal pay, and you will get virtually unanimous agreement. They are for it just as they are against sin."[97] Observers in the mid 1950s concluded that "sentiment in favor of equal pay is overwhelming."[98]

Tracing the language around the Equal Pay Bill reveals the dramatic roles played by its rhetorical content over the course of half a century. Depicted at first as a means of stifling job competition, it became a way of building the economy; shunned as a device to encourage individual ambition, it came to embody individual contributions to national well-being. Feared as a challenge to traditional gender roles, equal pay emerged as a way of enabling women to fulfill their family responsibilities; lauded as protection for men, it became a symbol of citizenship for women. As there was ambiguity in its early formulations and goals, so there remained ambiguity in its content even as it was passed into law. But the ambiguity was an essential ingredient in unifying diverse interests. Within its framework, the unresolved issue of occupational segregation remained hanging. And the ambiguity accounts as well for the fact that, in 1963, as the act was being debated on the House floor, it was gutted of language that required equal pay for "work of comparable quantity and quality" and that offered at least a restrained threat to labor market segregation.[99] This language, which had prevailed from World War II on, appeared in all legislative attempts to pass an equal pay bill until in the final debate it was removed from the legislation at the suggestion of one of its sponsors, Katharine St. George. Still, if the Equal Pay Act avoided challenges to this fundamental source of inequality in women's pay, it provided a rhetoric that fuelled a continuing struggle. The discourse expanded notions of justice, encouraging perceptions of male/female equality that had previously been invisible. Its limits and its achievements can be understood in terms of the hopes and fears that remained incarcerated in the term. Thus, it constitutes a case study of how close examination of rhetoric can help us understand some of the hidden dynamics of the political process.

5. The Just Price, the Free Market, and the Value of Women

I used to have a woman for a full day. But now they charge so much! We have to just make do. . . . Domestics make too much money now. You know, I'm a teacher and I don't make as much an hour as some domestics do. It's gotten all out of hand. . . . It's unskilled labor; you don't need training for it. Maybe there was a time when domestics weren't paid enough but now it's gotten to the opposite extreme. Do you think that's right? That an unskilled worker should make more than a teacher?"
—Chestnut Hill schoolteacher[1]

For feminist historians the 1980s could be described in the words with which Charles Dickens introduced *A Tale of Two Cities:* they were the best of times and the worst of times. On the one hand, the creative outpouring of historical scholarship on women became a source of energy and of continuing pressure for change. In the absence of a mass political movement, the enormous extension of historical knowledge (of which women's history remains the center), if it does nothing else, should ensure that women's orientations are permanently imprinted in the vocabulary of the past. But there is another hand: our sense of purpose seems to have wavered, our direction to be unclear. The feminist community no longer looks to history as the leading edge of scholarly research. Post-modern forms of literary criticism seem to have moved into that exalted rank. And even within the profession, women's history seems to have lost some of its shine as accusations of partisanship and fears of politicization limit our courage and restrict our vision.

And yet this is a moment when the voices of historians of women are needed more than ever. Some of the most significant social issues on the political agenda—family life, abortion, reproduction, and a range of issues having to do with economic equality—have a special meaning for women. As these become grist for legislative committees and judicial decisions, lawyers and policymakers increasingly invoke the past. In their hands the history of women emerges as something other than the product of historians. Women appear historically as well as philosophically "other," as a single, unified whole, instead of an amalgam of diverse experience.

A few examples will illuminate the issue. Feminist lawyers have disagreed sharply about whether to struggle for special treatment for women in the work force or to opt for equal treatment with men. In 1986 and 1987, the argument focused on pregnancy disability leaves. In the case of the *California Federal Savings and Loan Association* v. *Mark Guerra et al.* (commonly known as the *CalFed* case), the U.S. Supreme Court upheld a state law that provided such leaves for women without providing comparable time off for disabled men. Feminists, who came down on both sides, agreed in repudiating protective labor legislation that "classified men and women based on stereotypical notions of their sex roles." But they differed dramatically on the message of the past. One side drew a parallel between pregnancy disability legislation and the discredited protective laws, arguing that special treatment for women had distorted the contours of the labor force, encouraging employers to discriminate against them and contributing to occupational segregation in the labor market. Opposing lawyers insisted that a law that provided pregnancy leaves differed from earlier legislation in that it focused on "how women's unique reproductive role affects them in the work place." Pregnancy disability laws would not repeat the history of discrimination, this group suggested, but would, instead, enhance the possibility of achieving equality for women.[2]

In a second 1987 decision, the Supreme Court sustained the affirmative action plan of Santa Clara County, California. The plan included gender among the qualifications an employer could consider in assessing candidates for promotion and hiring. The majority affirmation of this moderate plan evoked a blistering dissent from Justice Antonin Scalia who called attention to the central issue underlying such cases: "It is a traditionally segregated job category," he noted of the road dispatcher's job in question, "*not* in the Weber sense, but in the sense that, because of longstanding social attitudes, it has not been regarded *by women themselves* as desirable work." Scalia followed this up with his own historical commentary: "There are, of course, those who believe that the social attitudes which cause women themselves to avoid certain jobs and to favor others are as nefarious as conscious, exclusionary discrimination. Whether or not that is so . . . the two phenomena are certainly distinct."[3] With all due respect to Justice Scalia, his description of these "two phenomena" reflects a historical consciousness to which many of us might object. Are conscious discrimination and social attitudes so easily separated? We once called this the difference between long-range and immediate causes.

A third example comes from an interview on comparable worth that appeared recently in the magazine *New Perspectives*, published by the U.S. Civil Rights Commission. The commission has in the last several years been an outspoken opponent of most forms of affirmative action and of all forms of comparable worth. "We do not have massive evidence that there was wage discrimination against women over the past one hundred years," commented the interviewer, an editor of the magazine, "so why should we now pass legislation or have a court make a ruling that assumes that the difference between men and women is due to discrimination?"[4] Does anyone dispute the fact that invidious distinctions between men and women are deeply rooted in the history of women's work? What "massive evidence" would satisfy this interviewer?

These examples illustrate how public or popular conceptions of the past can construct the future. They remind us that we have a responsibility as scholars to speak to public issues—to shape the visible perception of a past whose contours we have so fundamentally altered. They suggest that history, as a way of thinking, speaks to these issues, whether we, as individuals, will it or not, and therefore plays a crucial role in forming consciousness. A concern with contemporary issues enhances our capacity to think about the theoretical implications of the concrete empirical data in which we are immersed. Attention to historical reality encourages public policymakers to consider context, particularity, and diversity in the formulation of issues. A reciprocal relationship between history and public policy thus strengthens both areas, each on its own terms. And it offers us as historians of women a way of enhancing women's understanding of our womanly traditions.

I want to illustrate how this dialogue might work by looking at one of the burning issues of the day: pay equity or comparable worth. A major tenet of the feminist demand for equality is equity, or fairness, or justice. The demand underlines affirmative action programs and equal pay slogans. But what is equity in the job market? Like surrogate motherhood, homework, and pregnancy disability leaves, the pay equity strategy evokes contrary responses among feminists as well as antifeminists. Antifeminists suggest that it could increase labor conflict, worsen America's international competitive posture, and encourage a destructive female independence that will finally destroy the patriarchal family. Feminists who dismiss these arguments worry that it might nevertheless produce a host of evils including ghettoization in segregated occupations, economic inflation, expanded female unemployment, and increased female welfare dependency.

But comparable worth is clearly on the nation's political agenda. More than twenty states have some legislation that favors it; the 1984 Democratic party platform supported it; the AFL-CIO and several of its constituent unions have made it a priority issue. Minnesota has already implemented it for state jobs. The state of Washington is well on the way to doing so. Yet proponents and opponents of comparable worth differ sharply as to its justice or fairness.

Proponents suggest that the need for equity is self-evident. As one study observed, "The work women do is paid less, and the more an occupation is dominated by women, the less it pays."[5] That, they say, is manifestly unfair. But they disagree as to the basis for paying women more. Some argue that "jobs that are equal in value to the organization ought to be equally compensated whether or not the work content is similar."[6] Others suggest that the inequity resides in the market's failure to pay women a fair return on the human capital they have invested in the job.[7] Each calls on a different perception of history to solve two seemingly intractable historical problems facing women who earn wages: persistent occupational segregation and the stubborn wage gap between female and male workers. On the theory that low wages inhere in the job, which is itself sex-typed, advocates of comparable worth posit two central assumptions: first, that the free market has not worked for women, and second, that every job has an inherent value that can be compared with that of other jobs. Value, according to proponents of comparable worth, can be measured by such factors as the skill, effort, responsibility, training, and working conditions that are its requisites.

Critics ridicule the notion that value inheres in jobs. The market, they suggest—the demand for labor and the available supply—determines the wage paid. If women are not paid well, it is because they have made bad choices. And if these choices are historically conditioned, why should employers be held responsible? The language they use indicates something of the fear the idea evokes. Phrases like "the looniest idea since loony tunes" and "the feminist road to socialism" are the catchwords of the day.[8]

The historian hears these arguments impatiently, for whatever the abstract models proffered by economists, the historical record introduces the balm of experience. The market, as it functions in the daily lives of people, is not independent of the values and customs of those who participate in it. Justice, equity, and fairness have not been its natural outcomes. Rather, market outcomes have been tempered by customary notions of justice or fairness. The specific forms these take have been the object of struggle. And just as ideas of fairness influence our response to the market, so, too, do they influence how the market works.

Such notions go back to the earliest days of commerce. In the eleventh century, churchmen developed accepted notions of "just price" to resist an incipient market. Trying to avoid the inevitable disruption of traditional relationships that would occur if scarce labor were able, by means of restricting supply, to raise wages above those appropriate for its station, the church and the schoolmen who interpreted doctrine argued for an objective assessment of value. Measured by fair exchange or an equivalence of labor, value (and therefore price) inhered in every article of commerce and in the wage of every worker. Trade, in the minds of Thomas Aquinas and Albertus Magnus, might be a necessary evil, but it should be engaged in within the "customary estimate." Departure from that norm infringed on both religious and moral codes.

From the beginning the notion of just price embodied a subjective judgment. Since an important component of the wage and the price of the commodity to be sold was determined by the extent of the laborer's needs, just price rested on medieval conceptions of social hierarchy. "It corresponded," in the words of one economic historian, "to a reasonable charge that would enable the producer to support his family on a scale suitable to his station in life."9 Economic historians still debate the extent to which that correspondence emerged from the "common estimate" or market value of an object; but everyone agrees that a complex array of exchange factors mingled with a sense of propriety to form the final price. Thus, in one sense, just price was a subterfuge that enabled public authority to regulate an emerging market.

Whatever the weaknesses of just price theory and its rootedness in the moral concerns of the church, it passed down a continuing notion that nonmarket notions have a place in the valuation of objects or wage rates. In a period of labor shortages, notions of just price restricted the wages of labor and prevented skilled workers from banding together in what were labeled "conspiracies." When labor shortages gave way to surpluses, and the consensual wage that had been used to keep wages down began to decline, craftsmen and laborers (sometimes organized in guilds) resorted to just price theory to maintain a floor under wages. And as just price began to break down in the fifteenth century when the market expanded, notions that the wage ought to reflect some sense of need, rather than merely supply, lingered on. Its components are visible in the market system that emerged in the fifteenth century and reached full flower by the nineteenth. The customary wage, the wage demanded by the craftsperson or laborer, reflected a social sense of how a worker should live, as well as of the amount of labor that entered into the product for sale. We have not yet abandoned these notions. Changing ideas of fariness are implicit in our evaluation of the market and influence the way we impose taxes and otherwise regulate its outcomes.

In the free market, theoretically, demand and supply determine price. But in practice, wage theorists recognize a variety of what Harvard professor and former Secretary of Labor John Dunlop has called "exterior" factors in determining the wage.[10] These exterior factors are influences on the labor market that emerge from nonmarket factors like union contracts, seniority systems, and a sense of equity. Contemporary wage theorists have elaborate ways of describing how the market is restricted by these historical tendencies. Arthur M. Ross argues that wages move in what he calls "orbits of coercive comparison." This is simply another way of saying that traditional market forces do not have "compelling significance" in the determination of wages.[11] Rather, wages are influenced by the force of ideas about justice and equity and the power of organizations and individuals to sustain them. In this widely accepted model, workers compare their wages to those of other workers; pride and dignity prevent them from settling for less than their peers are getting. Other economists talk about "job clusters": firemen insist on parity with police; steelworkers strike to maintain equivalent wages nationwide, though in fact the market could easily pay less in some areas of the country. All these ideas and the social sensibilities that sustain them limit or modify market wages.

According to Ross, workers use comparisons to establish the dividing line between a "square deal and a raw deal." In a competitive market where most workers do not leave jobs for wages but are promoted from within and rely on the job for security, a worker might not earn what he would like; but as Ross put it, "he wants what is coming to him. . . . [It is] . . . an affront to his dignity and a threat to his prestige when he receives less than another worker with whom he can *legitimately* be compared."[12] I leave hanging for the moment the gendered content of "legitimately."

If wages reflect the relationship between some workers and others, they also tell us something about the relation between the craftsperson and the object produced, between the laborer and the employer, and among employers as well. Autoworkers, for example, agree that productivity and profits are appropriate factors to consider when determining the wage. They demand a share in the distribution of profits in good years and may reluctantly accept cutbacks in bad ones. Similarly, employers refuse wage increases that would raise the standard in an industry, even when their own profits make such raises possible. "Wage rates," as economist Michael Piore suggests, "perform certain basic social and institutional functions. They define relationships between labor and management, between one group of workers and another . . . and . . . [they define] the place of individuals relative to one another in the work community, in the neighborhood, and in the family."[13]

Because wages function, like the labor market itself, to structure relationships, comparable worth provides a parallel rather than a substitute strategy for achieving equity. Some feminists criticize comparable worth on the grounds that it will ghettoize women. The wage, they suggest, is a function of jobs held, and the proper remedy for women who want equal wages is to seek access to traditionally male jobs where the pay is better. After all, the argument goes, affirmative action legislation, now in place, will open up the market to women's labor and eliminate the main cause of the wage gap: occupational segregation. The Equal Pay Act of 1963 will then insure that women are treated equally. Fighting for affirmative action increases women's admission to male bastions and, by encouraging them to act on male conceptions of the market, will secure for them permanent access to the best jobs.

But, like the wage, the labor market is itself a regulating device, the product of a long history of social relationships heavily influenced by traditional conceptions of gender roles. While abstract market goals indicate that people *choose* jobs, the historical record suggests that occupational segregation has been the product of deeply ingrained attitudes. What appears to be a "natural" consequence of women's social roles has to be measured against the specific shape of occupational segregation at a given historical moment. Ideas about women "following" jobs into the marketplace, or choosing jobs that fill nurturing roles, or preferring to satisfy some abstract social ethic rather than to make money, are all ways of rationalizing nonmarket behavior by means of some other notion of equity. These and other specific social customs help legitimize the continuing and changing shape of the labor market. But they are and have been the frequent subject of negotiation and challenge by women. The historian who explores the workings of the labor market and reads complaints about its rigidities in particular times and places learns how segmentation functioned at certain moments and contributes to understanding the way in which gender roles have helped to construct the market as well.

Notions of craft and brotherhood, of masculinity and femininity, are embedded in and confirmed by the labor market, raising questions as to the definition of justice embodied in a "free labor market" in which inclusion and exclusion are a function of many things—including sex. Even a cursory glance at the rationalizations employers and managers have used to regulate women's participation leaves no doubt that the labor market has been socially, not abstractly, constructed. Thus, particular notions of equity are expressed by the London guilds that declared in the fourteenth century that "no man of the trade should set any woman to work other than his wife and daughter."[14] Medieval injunctions are echoed by those of many trade unions and male workplaces in our own time. As late as the 1960s and 1970s, employers explained why they had no women in certain jobs by calling upon customary ideas. "The nature of the work [did] not lend itself to employment in production of either women or the handicapped," said one wire manufacturer in 1973. And a pharmaceutical manufacturer told an interviewer in 1968 that they would hire women in clerical occupations and elsewhere "where the physical requirements of the task involved do not preclude it."[15] Such social attitudes continue down to this moment to serve as guides to what is equitable in the labor market. A 1987 cover story in *Business Week* notes that women "are being promoted because they bring new management styles to the corporation. According to the article, experts report "that female personality traits such as an ability to build consensus and encourage participation are in demand today. . . . women typically show more warmth and concern about human relationships and human sensitivities."[16] And when such qualities go out of fashion will women be demoted?

We begin now to see why the idea of comparable worth is so threatening. Just price theory imbued the market with a sense of equity that serves as a compelling (if sometimes unpredictable) influence on it. But whose sense of equity? An important element of equity, itself historically rooted, is a subjective evaluation of gender roles. A customary wage—a wage that reflects a social sense of how men and women should and do live—is partially an effort to preserve the status quo. Because the customary wage was built on a sense of the family as economic unit, it incorporated and passed down prevailing conceptions of gender. Because it was tied to continuing social hierarchy and women's restricted place, it affirmed women's secondary positions. Thus, "a woman's wage" has long been a term of opprobrium among men. A male worker could not legitimately be compared with a female worker without violating his sense of dignity and justice. Nor did the sense of justice of most female workers historically require such comparisons.

But times have changed, and along with them our conceptions of justice are altering. As E.H. Carr put it, abstractions "are indispensable categories of thought but they are devoid of meaning or application till specific content is put into them." Like checks drawn on a bank, "the printed part consists of abstract words like liberty and equality, justice and democracy . . . valueless until we fill in the other part, which states how much liberty we propose to allocate to whom, whom we recognize as our equals and up to what amount. The way we fill in the cheque from time to time is a matter of history."[17] Many (but never all) women in the past accepted a model of equity in the labor market based on the ideology of the patriarchal family. Most arguments for female equality derived from male conceptions of justice and were debates about access, not about new rules. New material conditions have shifted the content of equity from a demand for equality with men to a challenge to male structures. The altered terms of the debate no longer ask how women can achieve equality in a predominantly male work world so much as how to revalue the world of work and workers in a way that incorporates female self-interest. Rooted not in the moral economy of the male, but in the traditions, customs, and practices of women, the idea of comparable worth evokes a history that assesses the changing sense of right or dignity on which people will act.

That sense emerges from a historical context that alters definitions of what people are willing to accept. Disruptive conditions of early industrialization framed nineteenth century arguments for a male wage sufficient to keep wives out of the work force. Early twentieth century battles for a wage adequate to sustain women who were not secondary earners reflected a mature industrial economy in which women had essential but apparently temporary roles as wage laborers. The U.S. Women's Bureau fought bitterly to defend protective labor legislation in the 1920s—a battle rooted in historically conditioned understandings of women's primary task as childbearers and rearers. By the mid twentieth century, campaigns for equal pay for equal work reflected a shift in notions of equity rooted in the job to be performed rather than in an abstract conception of women's roles. Within the last ten years, the increasing pauperization of women and children in the United States has become a major incentive to redistribute income and thus an important argument for comparable worth. The campaign for pay equity reflects this new historical stage: because both men and women are recognized providers, the search for equity now includes a demand that jobs be evaluated on their own terms. Changing family structures have clearly played a political part in encouraging a revaluation of women's economic roles. The emergence of the argument is itself an indication that the conception of justice that underlined the legitimacy of a woman's wage is now called into question.

Like other redefinitions of equity, the consequences of this one are not self-evident. Thus, we argue over whether struggles for the family wage in the nineteenth century reflected women's interests in stable family life or men's desire to push women out of the labor market; over whether the capacity of women to earn wages yielded independence and autonomy or served to extend family obligations. Each stage reflects a social transformation that delegitimized certain customary roles and replaced them with others and from which some women benefited while others did not. And so it is with the struggle for pay equity for women. We can and must debate the way it will affect particular groups of women within a context that observes the social transformation of which the demand is a part.

Comparable worth now appears as part of a long political process within which women have tried to achieve some sense of equity and justice as it is defined in their historical period. Why then is it so strongly resisted? In part, I suggest, because a large and potentially powerful group of wage earners in questioning the conception of the free market, challenges its ideological roots as well. Because it raises to consciousness the issue of equity on which the market rests, comparable worth challenges the legitimacy of gender lines. It purports to delegitimize one element of the market pattern, namely sex. The end result would be to equate male and female workers, to threaten a male worker's sense of self, pride, and masculinity, and to challenge the legitimacy of basic institutions that touch all aspects of social and political life. The federal district court that rejected the request of Denver nurses that they be paid as much as the city's tree trimmers caught the problem exactly. Such a change, the court commented in a much-quoted decision, "was pregnant with the possibility of disrupting the entire economic system of the United States."[18]

The point is that it might be true. In refusing to acknowledge the legitimacy of gender distinctions, comparable worth raises a long line of earlier challenges to a new level. The historical context reveals pay equity to be both an issue of the gendered definition of justice and of the way justice manifests itself in the market. Seen from that perspective, comparable worth calls for nothing less than the revaluation of women. Its strength lies in its potential for acting upon female traditions, for it assumes that women have a right to pursue traditional roles and to achieve equity in that pursuit. Thus, it sustains those qualities of womanhood—nurture, community, and relational abilities—that are likely to have been products of women's cultural and social roles and have, as a result, been traditionally devalued by the job market.

But comparable worth poses one other crucial challenge to historians. Because it rests on a redefinition of equity, which is historically specific, it confronts us with definitions of difference that are rooted in historical experience. The debate over comparable worth thus opens the question of what difference has meant to various groups of women and how it has manifested itself. The task is crucial to understanding changing forms of justice. If we allow abstract descriptions of "woman" and abstract notions of "woman's culture" to govern our interpretations of the past, we provide what E.H. Carr called a "blank cheque." We offer empty categories that invite ideological uses of the past. We have seen (in the case of the *Equal Employment Opportunity Commission* v. *Sears, Roebuck and Co.*) the consequences that this "blank cheque" can have in arguments that the nurturing and biological roles of all women preclude working women and needy women from seeking rewards in the work force, discourage them from investing in human capital, and lead them to devote more time and attention to families.[19] These arguments, which are partly sustained by appeals to recent philosophy and psychology of sex differences, and which rest on conceptions of the universal female, are negated by historical experience. Not that most women have not performed traditional tasks, but the history of women's actual work force roles demonstrates a far more complex set of struggles by which different women at different times and places have tried to find their own directions in their own ways. In the United States, immigrant women, educated women, black women, poor women, married and unmarried women have each in their own ways come to locate their places within the shifting bounds of historical possibility.

Notions of universal womanhood blind us to the reciprocally confirming relationship of the work force and gendered ideas of social role. Judith Long Laws talks about the labor market providing information that conditions aspiration and channels people's expectations along realistic paths.[20] The historical record reveals how readily information changes in wars and depressions, how selectively it is presented to poor women as opposed to those who are well off, how much more limited it is for women of color than for white women. It demonstrates that difference is not a universal category but a social specific. And it reveals that how women handle differences can vary dramatically with historical circumstance. Carole Turbin and Mary Blewett, among other scholars, offer evidence of "nondichotomous" differences.[21] They suggest that women can be different in terms of life patterns and family commitments and yet struggle in the work force like men and with them.

We are led to two conclusions. First, while social and cultural differences between men and women surely exist, their abstract expression is less instructive than clear-eyed analysis of it in historical context. Second, such analysis should not be allowed to obscure differences among women and the historically specific ways in which they manifest themselves and serve as sources of tension and change. Poet Audre Lorde put it this way: Difference, she argued, "must be not merely tolerated, but seen as a fund of necessary polarities between which our creativity can spark like a dialectic."[22]

In the labor market, difference provides the core of struggle. It is entrenched in the cultural symbolism of jobs. Outdoor, heavy, and skilled work are associated with pay/provider roles, while dexterity and compassion are tied to poor pay and secondary jobs. Difference is reflected as well in the struggle of men and women to maintain dependent as well as independent relationships. The working class husband who tells an interviewer that his wife "doesn't know how to be a real wife, you know, feminine and really womanly. . . . She doesn't know how to give respect because she's too independent. She feels that she's a working woman and she puts in almost as many hours as I do and brings home a paycheck, so there's no one person above the other. She doesn't want there to be a king in this household"[23] is saying something about his expectations of traditional roles that we need to hear. The women who opposed the Equal Rights Amendment because they feared giving up alimony are reluctant to abandon their conceptions of equity for new and unknown forms. But these are not universal statements. They are pieces of a historical struggle we need to understand. They tell us something about the distribution of rewards in a society and about the role that sexual constraints play in it, about the structure of power and about their gendered meanings. They therefore tell us something about the reciprocal relationship between sexuality and social power.

In negating individual and particular experience, abstract arguments from difference ride roughshod over the aspirations and motivations of most women. The undifferentiated "woman" becomes a reified object instead of a social category subject to analysis, an abstraction rather than an actor in the historical enterprise. This is not an argument against theory or against conceptualizing. Rather, it is a plea that our theories be conditioned by the experiences of real actors: an expression of concern that the "universal female" not become a device to negate the possibility of equity and inadvertently open the door to perpetual inequality.

We are brought full circle. History offers a picture of wage relations that are not systemic but constructed and processual—a picture from which most women were once excluded, and into which they are now drawn. Like the labor market itself, the wage relation is constructed out of the subjective experience and rests ultimately on the legitimacy of historically specific notions of gender "difference." The historical record puts teeth into arguments for pay equity. As part of a changing battle for a changing definition of justice, its political parameters become comprehensible, and the meaning of the argument becomes more apparent.

Comparable worth illustrates how we construct consciousness out of historical experience. And it illustrates as well how the historian who explores the past in dialogue with the present can develop a richer understanding of the past. The struggle of women to redefine concepts like justice, liberty, and power, which reflect a vision of the future, pushes us to explore the past from which such ideas emerged. Because ideas don't come from thin air, our attempts to discover how they took shape, how diverse groups appropriated, shaped, and rejected them, enrich our understanding of the historical process and place content into what is otherwise a blank check or an empty box.

The reverse is also true. Without a history, public policy follows the paths of social myth. By entering the debate, we, historians of women, have in our hands the possibility of shaping the future. Without a history, our argument that women have a right to paid work can be turned into an excuse to push women with small children to take poorly paid, meaningless jobs. Without a history, our search for safe and accessible methods of birth control can be (and has been) translated into forced sterilization for the most vulnerable among us. Without a history, it is plausible for policymakers, legislatures, New Right groups, and ordinary women to interpret the problems women encounter in doing paid jobs as products of personal "choices" rather than as social issues. Without a history, employed women are asked to find solutions to what are called their own personal problems in their own ways.

An influential pair of sociologists demonstrated the consequences of an obligingly absent historical consciousness this way: When "family obligations come to be perceived as obstacles to self-realization in [women's] careers, individual women will have to decide on their priorities. Our own hope is that many will come to understand that life is more than a career and that this 'more' is above all to be found in the family. But, however individual women decide, they should not expect public policy to underwrite and subsidize their life plans."[24] To which the historian of women, politely eschewing the temptation to tackle the false historical assumptions contained in the statement, responds that as long as policymakers can invent a history that ignores the rich diversity of women's experiences, our task will not be completed.

Notes

INTRODUCTION

1. Victoria Byerly, *Hard Times Cotton Mill Girls: Personal Histories of Womanhood and Poverty in the South* (Ithaca, N.Y.: ILR Press, 1986), 170.

2. Lillian Breslow Rubin, *Worlds of Pain: Life in the Working-Class Family* (New York: Basic Books, 1976), 174.

1. THE WAGE CONCEIVED

1. Henry A. Landsberger, *Hawthorne Revisited: Management and the Worker, Its Critics, and the Developments in Human Relations in Industry* (Ithaca, N.Y.: Cornell University, 1958), 19.

2. New York State, *Factory Investigating Commission*, Fourth Report (Albany: S.B. Lyon Co., 1915), vol. 1, app. 3, passim. (Hereinafter referred to as FIC.)

3. N. Arnold Tolles, *Origins of Modern Wage Theories* (Englewood Cliffs, N.J.: Prentice-Hall, 1964), 8.

4. This theory, known as marginal productivity theory, was predicated on the assumption of perfect competition and emphasized the demands of employers in calculating the wage. Its classic exposition is John Bates Clark, *The Distribution of Wealth* (New York: MacMillan, 1899).

5. FIC, Fourth Report, vol. 4, 435.

6. In the United States, organized workers agitated for the idea beginning in the 1830s.

7. Melton McLaurin, *Paternalism and Protest: Southern Cotton Mill Workers and Organized Labor, 1875-1905* (Westport, Conn.: Greenwood Press, 1971), 23, describes how the notion of a family wage that

rested on the labor of all family members could contribute to expectations of female and child labor. In southern textile mills, "mill management argued that the total annual income of a mill family was far greater than that of a farm family. Thus the 'family wage' was used as a cover for the low wages paid individuals" (23). But this is not the usual understanding. See Martha May, "The Historical Problem of the Family Wage: The Ford Motor Company and the Five Dollar Day," *Feminist Studies*, 8 (Summer 1982), 394-424.

8. For access to the opposing positions, see Jane Humphries, "The Working Class Family, Women's Liberation, and Class Struggle: The Case of Nineteenth Century British History," *Review of Radical Political Economics*, 9 (Fall 1977), 25-41; Michelle Barrett and Mary McIntosh, "The Family Wage: Some Problems for Socialists and Feminists," *Capital and Class*, 11 (1980), 51-72; and Hilary Land, "The Family Wage," *Feminist Review*, 6 (1980), 55-78.

9. John A. Ryan, *A Living Wage: Its Ethical and Economic Aspects* (New York: Macmillan, 1906), 117.

10. William Smart, *Studies in Economics* (London: Macmillan, 1985), 34. Smart added that "in addition perhaps some consumption of alcohol and tobacco, and some indulgence in fashionable dress are, in many places, so habitual that they may be said to be 'conventionally necessary'" (34).

11. Cited by Ryan, *Living Wage*, 130, from the *American Federationist*, 1898.

12. Ryan, *Living Wage*, 117.

13. Ibid., vii.

14. Italics mine. Quoted in May, "Historical Problem of the Family Wage," 402. Samuel Gompers believed the worker's living wage should "be sufficient to sustain himself and those dependent upon him in a manner to maintain his self-respect, to educate his children, supply his household with literature, with opportunities to spend a portion of his life with his family." In Samuel Gompers, "A Minimum Living Wage," *American Federationist*, 5 (April 1898), 26.

15. See, for example, the list compiled by F. Spencer Baldwin in Louise Bosworth, *The Living Wage of Women Workers* (New York: Longmans Green and Co., 1911), 7; see also Elizabeth Beardsley Butler, *Women and the Trades: Pittsburgh, 1907-1908* (Pittsburgh: University of Pittsburgh Press, 1984 [1909]), 346-47.

16. J. Laurence Laughlin, ed., *Principles of Political Economy by John Stuart Mill* (New York: D. Appleton and Company, 1885), 214.

17. Italics mine. Ryan, *Living Wage*, 107.

18. Lynn Y. Wiener, *From Working Girl to Working Mother: The Female Labor Force in the United States, 1820-1980* (Chapel Hill: University of North Carolina, 1985), 19, 26, 84.

19. Ryan, *Living Wage*, 107.

20. Ibid., 120.

21. Kellogg Durland, "Labor Day Symposium," *American Federationist* 12 (September 1905), 619.

22. Ryan, *Living Wage*, 107.

23. Ibid., 133.

24. Dorothy W. Douglas, *American Minimum Wage Laws at Work* (New York: National Consumers' League, 1920), 14.

25. Butler, *Women and the Trades*, 346; Bosworth, *Living Wage of Women Workers*, 9. The Women's Bureau estimated that the minimums in effect from 1913 to 1915 ranged from $8.50 to $10.74. See Bulletin no. 61, *The Development of Minimum Wage Laws in the United States: 1912-1927* (Washington, D.C.: Government Printing Office, 1928).

26. Thomas Herbert Russell, *The Girl's Fight for a Living: How to Protect Working Women from Dangers Due to Low Wages* (Chicago: M.A. Donahue, 1913), 108.

27. Elizabeth Brandeis, "Labor Legislation," vol. 3 of John Commons, *History of Labor in the United States* (New York: Macmillan, 1935), 524-25, makes the point that these budgets were calculated in one of two ways: on the basis of actual expenditures (a problem because women had to live on what they earned, however small) or on the basis of theoretical budgets (a problem because employer-members of boards resisted the inclusion of such items as recreation, "party dress," etc.). They were then "modified" by estimates of prevailing wages, consideration of the amounts of the proposed increases, and possible consequences for business conditions.

28. Sue Ainslee Clark and Edith Wyatt, "Working-Girls' Budgets: A Series of Articles Based upon Individual Stories of Self-Supporting Girls," *McClure's*, 35 (October 1910). Additional articles appeared in *McClure's* in vol. 36 in November and December 1910 and February 1911. They were published in book form under the title, *Making Both Ends Meet: The Income and Outlay of New York Working-Girls* (New York: Macmillan, 1911). The classic study is that of Louise Bosworth, cited above.

29. Clark and Wyatt, "Working-Girls' Budgets," *McClure's*, 35 (October 1910), 604. See the discussion of these budgets in Wiener, *From Working Girl to Working Mother*, 75-77; and Joanne Meyerowitz, *Wo-*

men Adrift: Independent Wage Earners in Chicago, 1880-1930 (Chicago: University of Chicago Press, 1988), 33-35.

30. The magazine advertised for contributions in January 1908 and published from four to six contributions from February 1908 to January 1909. In September 1908 it announced that it was flooded with contributions and would no longer accept any more. There is no way of knowing how heavily these were edited, so they have been used here only to extract a broad gauge of opinion.

31. "The Girl Who Comes to the City," *Harper's Bazar*, 42 (January 1908), 54.

32. "The Girl Who Comes to the City," 42 (October 1908), 1005; 42 (July 1908), 694.

33. "The Girl Who Comes to the City," 42 (August 1908), 776. The maximum achieved by any of these women was the $100 a month earned by a Washington D.C., civil servant (42 [November 1908], 1141). That sum was sufficient for a single woman not only to live reasonably well but to save and invest some of her income. It was rarely achieved by women.

34. "The Girl Who Comes to the City," 42 (November 1908), 1141; see also October 1908, 1007.

35. See, for example, Alice Kessler-Harris, *Out to Work: A History of Wage Earning Women in the United States* (New York: Oxford, 1982), 99-101; Meyerowitz, *Women Adrift*, 34-36.

36. "The Girl Who Comes to the City," 42 (March 1908), 277; 42 (May 1908), 500. The widespread nature of this assumption is apparent in "Women's Wages," *Nation*, 108 (February 22, 1919), 270-71: "The employer of women today is in a large proportion of cases heavily subsidized; for there is a considerable gap between the $9 a week that is paid to a girl and her actual cost of maintenance. Who makes up the difference? In the employer's mind it is usually the girl's family—which is often mythical."

37. Smart, *Studies in Economics*, 115.

38. Butler, *Women and the Trades*, 346.

39. Meyerowitz, *Women Adrift*, 33.

40. Butler, *Women and the Trades*, 344.

41. FIC, Fourth Report, vol. 4, app. 3, 450.

42. Scott Nearing, "The Adequacy of American Wages," *Annals of the American Academy of Political and Social Sciences*, 59 (May 1915), 122.

43. "Women's Wages and Morality," *American Federationist*, 20 (June 1913), 467.

44. Smart, *Studies in Economics*, 125.

45. Russell, *Girl's Fight for a Living*, 21. On pay differences by race, see Meyerowitz, *Women Adrift*, 36; and Dolores Janiewski, *Sisterhood Denied: Race, Gender and Class in a New South Community* (Philadelphia: Temple University Press, 1985), 110-13.

46. FIC, Fourth Report, vol. 2, app. 3, 468; Don D. Lescohier, then a Minnesota statistician and later to become an eminent gatherer of labor statistics, commented at the same hearings that "custom . . . plays a far larger part in holding wages stationary than we have been accustomed to think" (ibid., 459).

47. Smart, *Studies in Economics*, 116. The radical Scott Nearing, in a minority opinion, held that the male wage was not determined by another principle at all. He protested industry's lack of attention to social relations: "The man with a family is brought into active competition with the man who has no family obligations. The native-born head of a household must accept labor terms which are satisfactory to the foreign-born single man. Industry does not inquire into a worker's social obligations" (Nearing, "Adequacy of American Wages," 123).

48. Which is not, of course, to imply that all males who earned wages were paid enough to support families. See Janiewski, *Sisterhood Denied*, for illustrations of wages in the southern tobacco and textile industries that required the labor of three or more people to sustain a family.

49. Bosworth, *Living Wage*, 4.

50. Russell, *Girl's Fight for a Living*, 73.

51. Ibid., 108.

52. Ibid., 83.

53. Smart, *Studies in Economics*, 107.

54. Samuel Gompers, "Woman's Work, Rights and Progress," *American Federationist*, 20 (August 1913), 625.

55. Alfred Marshall, *Principles of Economics*, 8th ed. (New York: Macmillan, 1953), 685.

56. Quoted in Russell, *Girl's Fight for a Living*, 16; and see "Women's Wages and Morality," 465.

57. Russell, *Girl's Fight for a Living*, 38; cf. also the testimony of Ida Tarbell in ibid., 39.

58. Butler, *Women and the Trades*, 342-43.

59. Frances Amasa Walker, *The Wages Question: A Treatise on Wages and the Wages Class* (New York: Henry Holt and Company, 1876), 374.

60. Ibid., 378.

61. Quoted in Marjorie Shuler, "Industrial Women Confer," *Woman Citizen*, 8 (January 27, 1923), 25.

62. Such arguments were prefigured in the late nineteenth century by assertions that the greedy were taking jobs from the needy. See Kessler-Harris, *Out to Work*, 99ff.

63. "Women as Wage Earners," *New York Times*, January 28, 1923, 26.

64. Maurine Greenwald, *Women, War, and Work: The Impact of World War One on Women in the United States* (Westport, Conn.: Greenwood Press, 1980), 155. Greenwald notes that a female janitor who might have made $35 a month earned $75-80 a month as a conductor.

65. Daniel Nelson, *Managers and Workers: Origins of the New Factory System in the United States* (Madison: University of Wisconsin Press, 1975), 145.

66. Quoted in "Women and Wages," *The Woman Citizen*, 4 (June 7, 1919), 8. The article went on to report that one plant had "reckoned women's production as 20 per cent greater than that of the men preceding them. But this did not prevent the same plant from cutting down the women's pay one-third."

67. Typescript, "Memoranda Regarding Women's Bureau," in National Archives, Record Group 86, Box 4, File: WTUL Action on Policies. The bureau lost this battle. As a result, its professional staff tended to work more out of loyalty and commitment than for monetary gain. See Judith Sealander, *As Minority Becomes Majority: Federal Reaction to the Phenomenon of Women in the Work Force, 1920-1963* (Westport, Conn.: Greenwood Press, 1983), chap. 3, for the early days of the Women's Bureau.

68. Ronald W. Schatz, *The Electrical Workers: A History of Labor at General Electric and Westinghouse, 1923-60* (Urbana: University of Illinois Press, 1983), 32.

69. Quoted in Stephen Meyer III, *The Five Dollar Day: Labor Management and Social Control in the Ford Motor Company, 1908-1921* (Albany: State University of New York Press, 1981), 140.

70. Schatz, *Electrical Workers*, 20-21.

71. Quoted in Schatz, *Electrical Workers*, 21; Nelson, *Managers and Workers*, 118, confirms that the wage as welfare differed for men and women: "Manufacturers who employed large numbers of women usually emphasized measures to make the factory more habitable. Lunchrooms, restrooms, landscaping and other decorative features conveyed the idea of a home away from home. At the same time, the classes in domestic economy and child rearing, social clubs, outings

and dances (women only) assured the worker that she need not sacrifice her femininity when she entered the male world of the factory. But, because the female operative was (or was thought to be) a secondary wage earner and probably a transient, she was not offered pensions, savings programs and insurance plans."

72. Meyer, *Five Dollar Day*, 140; implicit in the Ford policy was a quite conscious attempt to circumscribe the roles and self-perceptions of men as well as of women. Meyer quotes a Ford policy manual from the 1920s to the effect that "if a man wants to remain a profit sharer, his wife should stay at home and assume the obligations she undertook when married" (141). See the commentary on this issue in "Housework Wages," *The Woman Citizen*, 4 (October 4, 1919), 449.

73. Russell, *Girl's Fight for a Living*, 101; the same investigator asked an employer, "If you raised a little girl from $3 to $8 would a man getting $15 feel aggrieved?" (112)—a question that loads the dice by imagining women as no more than children.

74. Microfilm records, Western Electric Plant, Hawthorne Works, Operating Branch M., interviews, Reel 6, July 8, 1929. Records of individuals are not identified or tagged beyond the branch where the interviews were taken. The growing sense of entitlement to comparable wages was captured by an experienced female worker who declared herself satisfied with her work "because it was more interesting and I could make my rate" but nevertheless complained that "I don't see why they didn't raise me anyway like they did the other girls, every half year or every year." In ibid., July 9, 1929. This phenomenon was not specific to women alone. F. J. Roethlisberger and William Dickson, analyzing the Western Electric research, commented, "The results of the interviewing program show very clearly that the worker was quite as much concerned with these differentials, that is the relation of his wages to that of other workmen as with the absolute amount of his wages." See *Management and the Worker: An Account of a Research Program Conducted by the Western Electric Company, Hawthorne Works, Chicago* (Cambridge, Mass.: Harvard University Press, 1946), 543. But nothing in the interviews indicates that women compared their wages with those of men, nor did men with those of women.

75. Mary Schaill and Ethel Best to Mary Anderson, November 5, 1919, Virginia Survey, Bulletin no. 10, National Archives, Record Group 86: Records of the Women's Bureau, Box 2.

76. Pauline Newman, veteran trade unionist, challenged old notions of a living wage in "The 'Equal Rights' Amendment," *American*

Federationist, 45 (August 1938), 815. She wrote, "It is not a wage which affords an opportunity for intellectual development; it is not a wage which allows for spiritual growth; it is not a wage on which wage-earning women can enjoy the finer things of life."

77. Ronald Edsforth, *Class Conflict and Cultural Consensus: The Making of a Mass Consumer Society in Flint, Michigan* (New Brunswick, N.J.: Rutgers University Press, 1987), 95.

78. Daniel T. Rodgers, *The Work Ethic in Industrial America: 1850-1920* (Chicago: University of Chicago Press, 1974), 196.

79. Theresa Wolfson, *The Woman Worker and the Trade Unions* (New York: International Publishers, 1926), 42.

80. Microfilm records, Western Electric Plant, Hawthorne Works, Operating Branch M., interviews, Reel 6, July 8, 1929.

81. Wolfson, *Woman Worker*, 42-43.

82. Microfilm records, Western Electric Plant, Hawthorne Works, Operating Branch M., interviews, Reel 6, Folder 1, Box 14, July 1, 1929.

83. Mary Anderson, "Industrial Standards for Women," *American Federationist*, 32 (July 1925), 565.

84. Jacquelyn Dowd Hall et al., *Like a Family: The Making of a Southern Cotton Mill World* (Chapel Hill: University of North Carolina Press, 1987), 255-56.

85. See interviews with Ada Mae Wilson, Mary Ethel Shockley, Ina Wrenn, and Gertrude Shuping in Southern Oral History Project Collection, Martin Wilson Library, University of North Carolina, Chapel Hill. Used with the kind help of Jacquelyn Dowd Hall.

86. The quotation is from FIC, Fourth Report, vol. 4, 440. The percentage of married black women working and supporting families was far higher than that for white women.

87. Shuler, "Industrial Women Confer," 12.

2. LAW AND A LIVING

This essay originated in the Conference on Women and the Progressive Period, sponsored by the Smithsonian Institution and the American Historical Association in March 1988.

1. Quoted in Florence Kelley, *Women's Work and War*, 1 (July 1918), 3.

2. The other states were Arizona, Arkansas, California, Colorado, Kansas, Massachusetts, Minnesota, North Dakota, Oregon, Texas, Utah, Washington, and Wisconsin. Bills were under consideration in Missouri, Ohio, New Jersey, and New York. For a summary of mini-

mum wage legislation to 1919, see Lindley D. Clark, "Minimum Wage Laws of the United States," *Monthly Labor Review*, 12 (March 1921), 1-20.

3. "Calls Wage Ruling by Court a Calamity," *New York Times*, April 12, 1923, 11. And see "The Minimum Wage Law," editorial, *New York Times*, April 11, 1923, 20; and "Freedom of Contract," *St. Louis Post-Dispatch*, April 10, 1923, 18. For contrary opinions with different reasoning, see "The Minimum Wage Decision," *Milwaukee Journal*, April 10, 1923, 8; and "The Minimum Wage Decision," *Washington Post*, April 10, 1923, 6.

4. "Minimum Wage Law for Women Is Void," *New York Times*, April 10, 1923, 23.

5. *New York World*, April 11, 1923, 13.

6. "New Wage Decision Stirs Women to Act," *New York Times*, April 11, 1923, 13.

7. "Labor Leaders Hit Wage Law Decision," *New York Times*, May 16, 1923, 5; and "Gompers Assails Wage Decision as Reactionary," *St. Louis Post-Dispatch*, April 10, 1923, 1.

8. Henry R. Seager, "The Minimum Wage: What Next? A Symposium," *Survey*, 50 (May 15, 1923), 216.

9. "Mr. Untermyer on the Minimum Wage Decision," *American Federationist*, 30 (May 1923), 408; see also opinions quoted by Seager in "The Minimum Wage: What Next?"; Barbara Grimes, "Comment on Cases," *California Law Review*, 11 (1923), 361; and "Minimum Wage Ruling Attacked," *New York Evening Post*, April 10, 1923, 1.

10. *Muller* v. *Oregon*, 208 U.S. 412 (1908).

11. The phrase is quoted from *Adkins* v. *Children's Hospital*, 261 U.S. 525 (1923), 546. For background see Judith Baer, *The Chains of Protection: The Judicial Response to Women's Labor Legislation* (Westport, Conn.: Greenwood Press, 1978); Susan Lehrer, *Origins of Protective Labor Legislation for Women: 1905-1925* (Albany, N.Y.: SUNY Press, 1987); and Elizabeth Faulkner Baker, *Protective Labor Legislation with Special Reference to Women in the State of New York*, Columbia University Studies in History, Economics, and Public Law, 116 (New York: Columbia University Press, 1925).

12. *Stettler v. O'Hara*, 243 U.S. 629 (1917).

13. Clark, "Minimum Wage Laws," 5; in addition to Oregon, the highest courts of Minnesota (*Williams* v. *Evans et al.*, 139 Minn. 32 [1917]); Arkansas (*State* v. *Crowe*, 130 Ark. 272 [1917]); Massachusetts (*Holcombe* v. *Creamer*, 231 Mass. 99 [1918]); and Washington (*Spokane Hotel* v. *Younger*, 113 Wash. 359 [1920]) had all explicitly sustained

such legislation. See Rome G. Brown, "Oregon Minimum Wage Cases," *Minnesota Law Review*, 1 (June 1917), 471-86.

14. In part, the relatively low level of opposition reflects the fact that many states excluded from coverage industries in which female labor was most crucial. For example, Texas excluded agriculture, domestic service, and nursing. Arkansas excluded cotton factories and fruit harvesting.

15. Baker, *Protective Labor Legislation*, 101-2, writing in 1924, raises the question as to whether this gender-based strategy might not in retrospect have been a mistake. After all, Sutherland struck down the law in part because, he argued, women were no longer different from men. And the Court had in *Bunting* v. *Oregon*, 243 U.S. 426 (1917), sustained a law protecting the health of male workers.

16. Cited in *Stettler* v. *O'Hara et al.*, 69 Ore. 519 (1914), 519; and in *Adkins* v. *Children's Hospital*, 525.

17. *Muller* v. *Oregon*, 422.

18. *Adkins* v. *Children's Hospital*, 546.

19. For the pre-Civil War notion, compare Eric Foner, *Free Soil, Free Labor, Free Men: The Ideology of the Republican Party before the Civil War* (New York: Oxford, 1970); for legal development in the gilded age, see William Forbath, "The Ambiguities of Free Labor: Labor and the Law in the Gilded Age," *Wisconsin Law Review* (1985), 767-817.

20. John B. Andrews and W.D.P. Bliss, *History of Women in Trade Unions* (New York: Arno Press, 1974 [1911]), 47, 48. Joan Scott has phrased the issue this way: "Since women were not considered to have property in labor," there was no solution to competition with men except to remove them from the labor force. "On Language, Gender, and Working-class History," *International Labor and Working Class History*, 31 (Spring 1987), 10.

21. The struggle is chronicled in such books as Leon Fink, *Workingmen's Democracy: The Knights of Labor and American Politics* (Urbana: University of Illinois Press, 1983); and Brian Greenberg, *Worker and Community: Response to Industrialization in a Nineteenth Century American City, Albany and New York, 1850-1884* (Albany: State University of New York Press, 1985).

22. Exceptions to a worker's right to freedom of contract generally included only such occupations as railroad workers, miners, and seamen where public health and safety were at risk. Where private health was concerned, as in the case of bakers and cigar makers, courts generally refused to support state intervention.

23. *Adkins* v. *Children's Hospital,* 554; this led one commentator to observe that "the idea of the opinion seems to be that somehow the Constitution entitles the employer to such benefits as he may derive from the independent resources of possible women employees" (Thomas Reed Powell, "The Judiciality of Minimum Wage Legislation," *Harvard Law Review,* 37 [1924], 565), which may not be literally the case, but which would certainly have been supported by prevailing notions of women's family roles. The effort to shake this false assumption was one of the goals of progressive reformers and is, as chap. 1 of this volume illustrates, repeated in much of the literature.

24. Leon Fink, "The New Labor History and the Powers of Historical Pessimism: Consensus, Hegemony, and the Case of the Knights of Labor," *Journal of American History,* 75 (June 1988), 115-36, argues that the idea of free labor retained much of its zest long after the corporate attack dropped. John Diggins, "Comrades and Citizens: New Mythologies in American Historiography," *American Historical Review,* 90 (June 1985), 614-38, argues in contrast that the corporate image won over most workers by the late 1880s. My own sense is that the issue of gender kept the question alive into the 1930s.

25. *Quong Wing* v. *Kirkendall,* 223 U.S. 59 (1912), 62.

26. Ibid., 63.

27. *Quong Wing* v. *Kirkendall,* 63. In a dissenting opinion, Justice Lamar denied that difference could be so arbitrarily used: "The individual characteristics of the owner do not furnish a basis in which to make a classification for purposes of taxation," he declared (64-65).

28. The best known case is, *Bradwell* v. *Illinois,* 16 Wall 130 (1873), in which Justice Miller, speaking for the Court, argued that the privileges and immunities protected by the Fourteenth Amendment did not supersede state laws—in this case the Illinois law that reserved membership in the bar to men. But it is Justice Bradley's concurring opinion that is widely cited, for Bradley chose to broaden the Illinois Supreme Court's assertion that Bradwell was properly deprived access to the bar because she was a *married* woman and thus could not be bound by contracts. According to Bradley, "the civil law has always recognized a wide difference in the respective spheres of man and woman. Man is, or should be, woman's protector and defender. The natural and proper timidity and delicacy which belongs to the female sex evidently unfits it for many of the occupations of civil life" (132). See also Leslie Friedman Goldstein, *The Constitutional Rights of Women: Cases in Law and Social Change* (New York: Longman, 1979), 45-51; Leo Kanowitz, *Sex Roles in Law and Society: Cases and Materials*

(Albuquerque: University of New Mexico Press, 1973), 42-46.

29. New York State, *Factory Investigating Commission*, Fourth Report, vol. 1 (Albany: S.B. Lyon Co., 1915), 25. (Hereinafter referred to as FIC.)

30. *Adkins* v. *Children's Hospital*, 555-56.

31. See the testimony of John Mitchell, Norman Hapgood, Edward Bates, and Albertus Nooner published in FIC, Fourth Report, vol. 1, 706, 769, 777, 780; and the testimony of Mary Simkhovitch, Frederick Whitin, and Martha Falconer in app. 3, 414, 410, 394.

32. *Morehead* v. *New York, ex rel Tipaldo*, 298 U.S. 587 (1936), 590.

33. Testimony of Harry Allen Overstreet and Roger Babson in FIC, Fourth Report, vol. 1, 730 and 790.

34. Crystal Eastman, "Equality or Protection," *Equal Rights*, 15 (March 1924), 156.

35. Testimony of Tim Healey and Homer Call in FIC, Fourth Report, vol. 1, 771, 770. Helen Marot (774) had an opposite perspective. And see William Green: "Women with centuries of homework and with traditions of legal wardship as a background do not find it as easy to establish voluntary collective bargaining with the employer as men workers," in "Equal Rights Amendment," *American Federationist*, 45 (March 1938), 245.

36. Testimony of Maude Miner, James Brown Reynolds, and Frederick Whitin, in FIC, Fourth Report, vol. 1, Appx. III, 410, 412, 416.

37. Testimony of Charles Augustus Yates, New York State, *Factory Investigating Commission, Syracuse Hearings* (Albany: S.B. Lyon, 1911), 1097.

38. Brown, "Oregon Minimum Wage Cases," 478.

39. Powell, "Judiciality of Minimum Wage Legislation," 545.

40. Martha Minow, "Rights in Relationship," unpublished paper, suggests that this dilemma might have been avoided by a relational view of the law that asks us to reimagine social relationships in wages that include the differences of some groups as parts of the community of interest instead of antithetical to it. While this offers a wonderful solution to some contemporary dilemmas, such a view in the early twentieth century would have vitiated freedom of contract altogether.

41. National Consumers' League, *The Supreme Court and Minimum Wage Legislation* (New York: New Republic, 1925), 204. Elizabeth Baker argued, "Both men and women need a living wage in order to live. A sub-living wage for men is perhaps the largest single cause of the entrance of their wives and children into gainful employment; thus the argument for prescribing the payment of a living wage by law

may prove to be as strong for one sex as for the other" (*Protective Labor Legislation*, 424-25).

42. *Adkins* v. *Children's Hospital*, 556.

43. *State* v. *Crowe*, 285.

44. Brief of Defendant in Error, U.S. Supreme Court, Records and Briefs, *Stettler* v. *O'Hara*, October term 1916-17, Docket no. 25 and 26, A12. And see testimony of Timothy Healey and Edward T. Devine, *FIC, Fourth Report*, vol. 1, 771, 697; as well as the discussion of these issues in Irwin Yellowitz, *Labor and the Progressive Movement in New York State, 1897-1916* (Ithaca: Cornell University Press, 1965), 131-35.

45. Ellis Brief, U.S. Supreme Court, Records and Briefs, *Adkins* v. *Children's Hospital*, October term 1922, Docket no. 795 and 796, 43.

46. Brown, "Oregon Minimum Wage Cases," 486.

47. Transcript of D.C. Supreme Court Opinion, June 6, 1921, U.S. Supreme Court, Records and Briefs, *Adkins* v. *Children's Hospital*, October term 1922, Docket no. 795 and 796, 42.

48. Van Orsdel opinion, *Adkins* v. *Children's Hospital*, 284 Fed. Rep. 613 (1922), 617.

49. Ibid., 621.

50. Ibid., 623.

51. This was countered by a supporter who argued, "If we fail to give adequate remedy to real oppressive conditions, the people will turn to other economic systems for remedies," State of Wisconsin, Amicus Curaie, Records and Briefs, *Adkins* v. *Children's Hospital*, 14).

52. Barbara H. Grimes, "Constitutional Law; Police Power; Minimum Wage for Women," in National Consumer's League, *Supreme Court and Minimum Wage Legislation*, 107.

53. *Adkins* v. *Children's Hospital*, 553.

54. *Adkins* v. *Children's Hospital*, 562; Taft's logic ran as follows: employees with the lowest pay are not equal to employers; they are subject to the overreaching of harsh and greedy employers; the result is the evils of the sweating system.

55. "Gompers Assails Wage Decision as Reactionary," *St. Louis Post-Dispatch*, April 10, 1923, 1.

56. In *Radice* v. *New York*, 264 U.S. 292 (1924), the Court sustained legislation that prohibited women from working at night. Other cases that turned back attempts to establish minimum wages included *Murphy* v. *Sardell*, 269 U.S. 530 (1925), re: Arizona; *Donham* v. *West Nelson Co.*, 273 U.S. 657 (1927), re: Arkansas; *Morehead* v. *New York, ex rel Tipaldo*, re: New York. For commentary on *Morehead*, see Robert L. Hale, "Minimum Wage and the Constitution," *Columbia Law Review*, 36 (April 1936), 629-33.

57. *West Coast Hotel Co.* v. *Parrish*, 300 U.S. 379 (1937), 391.

58. *West Coast Hotel Co.* v. *Parrish*, 399; note the shift in imagery here. Where earlier discussions had described women as a burden on the community, Hughes argued, "The community is not bound to provide what is in effect a subsidy for unconscionable employers" (399). Sutherland, dissenting, repeated at length his defense of freedom of contract as affirmed by Adkins, concluding somewhat plaintively, "We do not understand that it is questioned by the present decision" (406).

59. *West Coast Hotel Co.* v. *Parrish*, 400.

60. *West Coast Hotel Co.* v. *Parrish*, 399; Hughes quoted an earlier Court decision to the effect that "if the law presumably hits the evil where it is most felt, it is not to be overthrown because there are other instances to which it might have been applied" (400).

61. *United States* v. *Darby*, 312 U.S. 125 (1940); Kanowitz, *Sex Roles in Law and Society*, notes, "The cases relied on by the Court in Parrish were all cases that made no distinction between the sexes insofar as the constitutionality of the states' regulation of the employment relationship was concerned" (190). *West Coast Hotel Co.* v. *Parrish*, 393. Kanowitz also notes that the Court's decision in *Darby* signified its belief that in *Parrish* it had upheld a general minimum wage, not a minimum wage for women only (468).

62. *West Coast Hotel Co.* v. *Parrish*, 411, 412.

63. *Morehead* v. *New York*, 635.

3. PROVIDERS

This essay appeared in *Gender and History* 1 (Spring 1989):31-49. It appears here by permission of the publishers, Basil Blackwell.

1. Mrs. A.B. Grimm of Menasha, Wisconsin, to FDR, May 21, 1934, National Archives, Record Group 9: Records of the National Recovery Administration, Entry 23, Box 491. (Hereinafter referred to as NA RG 9.)

2. Earl A. Leiby to FDR, May 10, 1933, National Archives, Record Group 1974: General Records of the Department of Labor, Chief Clerk's Files, Entry 167/838, Box 183. (Hereinafter referred to as NA RG 174. All quotations are cited as in the original. Changes in the letters have been made only for the purposes of clarity.)

3. Blanche Crumbly to FDR, October 26, 1933, NA RG 9, Entry 398: Records relating to employee complaints in the textile industry,

Box 5, File: Bibb Manufacturing Co., Macon, Ga. (Hereinafter referred to as NA RG 9, Entry 398.)

4. The most coherent statement appears in Nancy Cott, *The Bonds of Womanhood: Woman's Sphere in New England, 1780-1835* (New Haven: Yale University Press, 1977), 67-74; see also Carroll Smith-Rosenberg, "The Female World of Love and Ritual: Relations between Women in Nineteenth Century America," and "The New Woman as Androgyne: Social Disorder and Gender Crisis, 1870-1936," in *Disorderly Conduct: Visions of Gender in Victorian America* (New York: Oxford University Press, 1986), 53-75, 245-96; Kathryn Kish Sklar, *Catharine Beecher: A Study in American Domesticity* (New Haven: Yale University Press, 1973); and Blanche Wiesen Cook, "Female Support Networks and Political Activism: Lillian Wald, Crystal Eastman, Emma Goldman," *Chrysalis*, 3 (1977), 43-62.

5. See the essays in Ruth Milkman, ed., *Women, Work and Protest: A Century of Women's Labor History* (London: Routledge and Kegan Paul, 1985), including Ardis Cameron, "Bread and Roses Revisited: Women's Culture and Working-Class Activism in the Lawrence Strike of 1912," 42-61; and Collette Hyman, "Labor Organizing and Female Institution Building: The Chicago Women's Trade Union League, 1904-1924," 22-41. See also, Dana Frank, "Housewives, Socialists and the Politics of Food: The New York Cost of Living Protests," *Feminist Studies*, 11 (Summer 1985), 255-85.

6. Linda Kerber, "Separate Spheres, Female Worlds, Woman's Place: The Rhetoric of Women's History," *Journal of American History*, 75 (June 1988), 11.

7. Nancy Hewitt, "Beyond the Search for Sisterhood: American Women's History in the 1980s," *Social History*, 10 (October 1985), 299-322.

8. Ellen DuBois et al., "Patterns and Culture in Women's History: A Symposium," *Feminist Studies*, 6 (Spring 1980), 26-64.

9. I am here following the definition of Frances E. Olsen: "A dichotomy exists when a significant aspect of experience is divided sharply between two categories that are mutually exclusive but together account for the entire aspect." See "The Family and the Market: A Study of Ideology and Legal Reform," *Harvard Law Review*, 96 (May 1983), 1498.

10. Ruth Milkman, *Gender at Work: The Dynamics of Job Segregation by Sex during World War II* (Urbana: University of Illinois Press, 1987), offers an excellent example of how this happened.

11. Leslie Woodcock Tentler, *Wage-Earning Women: Industrial*

Work and Family Life in the United States, 1900-1930 (New York: Oxford University Press, 1979); Susan Porter Benson, *Counter Cultures: Saleswomen, Managers, and Customers in American Department Stores, 1890-1940* (Urbana: University of Illinois Press, 1986); Barbara Melosh, *'The Physician's Hand': Work, Culture and Conflict in American Nursing* (Philadelphia: Temple University Press, 1982); Alice Kessler-Harris, *Out to Work: A History of Wage-Earning Women in the United States* (New York: Oxford University Press, 1982). See also, Louise Lamphere, *From Working Daughters to Working Mothers: Immigrant Women in a New England Industrial Community* (Ithaca, N.Y.: Cornell University Press, 1987); and Sallie Westwood, *All Day, Every Day: Factory and Family in the Making of Women's Lives* (Urbana: University of Illinois Press, 1985).

12. Dorothy Sue Cobble, "'Practical Women': Waitress Unionists and the Controversies over Gender Roles in the Food Service Industry, 1900-1980," *Labor History*, 29 (Winter 1988), 5-31; Alice Kessler-Harris, "Problems of Coalition Building: Women and Trade Unions in the 1920s," in Milkman, *Women, Work and Protest*, 110-38. Stephen Norwood, *Flaming Youth: Telephone Operators and Industrial Militancy* (Urbana: University of Illinois Press, forthcoming).

13. Dorothy Sue Cobble, "Working Class Female Perspectives on Gender Equality: Waitress Unionists in the Twentieth Century," unpublished paper delivered at the meeting of the Organization of American Historians, Reno, Nevada, April 1988. Cited by permission.

14. Mary Blewett, *Men, Women, and Work: Class, Gender, and Protest in the New England Shoe Industry, 1780-1910* (Urbana: University of Illinois Press, 1988).

15. Carole Turbin, "Beyond Dichotomies: Interdependence in Mid-Nineteenth Century Working Class Families in the United States," *Gender and History* 1, (Autumn 1989): 293-308.

16. Charles Sabel, *Work and Politics: The Division of Labor in Industry* (Cambridge and New York: Cambridge University Press, 1892), 80.

17. I am drawing here on a formulation offered by Michael Piore in "Labor Market Segmentation: To What Paradigm Does It Belong?" unpublished paper delivered at the American Economic Association meetings, New York, 1982, 13.

18. For a critique of Thompson in relationship to gender, see Joan Wallach Scott, "Women in *The Making of the English Working Class*," in *Gender and the Politics of History* (New York: Columbia University Press, 1988), 68-90.

19. David Montgomery, *Workers' Control in America: Studies in the*

History of Work, Technology and Labor Struggles (New York: Cambridge University Press, 1979), 13-14.

20. Some of these are discussed in Patricia Cooper, *Once a Cigar Maker: Men, Women and Work Culture in American Cigar Factories, 1900-1919* (Urbana: University of Illinois Press, 1987), 321-23.

21. Linda Frankel, "Southern Textile Workers: Generations of Survival and Struggle," in Karen Brodkin Sacks and Dorothy Remy, eds., *My Troubles Are Going to Have Trouble with Me: Everyday Trials and Triumphs of Women Workers* (New Brunswick, N.J.: Rutgers University Press, 1984), 46. For a discussion of other perceptions on which women might have acted in the 1920s, see Kessler-Harris, "Problems of Coalition Building."

22. See, especially, Ardis Cameron, "Bread and Roses Revisited," in Milkman, *Women, Work and Protest;* Carole Turbin, "Reconceptualizing Family, Work and Labor Organizing: Working Women in Troy, 1860-1890," *Review of Radical Political Economics,* 16 (Spring 1984), 1-16; and Michael Kazin's critique of David Montgomery's *The Fall of the House of Labor,* in *Labor History,* 30 (Winter 1989), 110-13.

23. Sally Alexander, "Women, Class and Sexual Difference," *History Workshop,* 17 (Spring 1984), 125-49.

24. Warren Susman, "The Culture of the Thirties," in *Culture and Commitment: The Transformation of American Society in the Twentieth Century* (New York: Pantheon, 1984); U.S. Department of Labor, Women's Bureau, *Women Workers and Family Support,* Bulletin no. 49 (Washington, D.C.: Government Printing Office, 1925).

25. Lois Scharff, *To Work and to Wed: Female Employment, Feminism, and the Great Depression* (Westport, Conn.: Greenwood Press, 1980); Susan Ware, *Holding Their Own: American Women in the 1930s* (Boston: Twayne, 1982).

26. The Women's Bureau estimated that 1,603 federal employees lost their jobs between June 30, 1932, and December 31, 1934. U.S. Department of Labor, Women's Bureau, "Gainful Employment of Married Women" (mimeographed pamphlet, 1936), Martin Catherwood Library, Cornell University, American Association for Labor Legislation Collection, Box: Women. And see Ruth Milkman, "Women's Work and the Economic Crises: Some Lessions from the Great Depression," *Review of Radical Political Economics,* vol. 8 (Spring 1976), 73-97; Alice Kessler- Harris, *Out to Work: A History of Wage-Earning Women in the United States* (New York: Oxford University Press, 1982), ch. 9; Julia Kirk Blackwelder, *Women of the Depression:*

Caste and Culture in San Antonio, 1929-1939 (College Station: Texas A & M University Press, 1984).

27. E.E. Jett to FDR, June 23, 1933, NA RG 174, Entry 167/838, Box 183. Jett described his letter as "the bravest thing I have ever tried" and concluded it with, "Will you reply to this, PLEASE."

28. William Launder to Louis Howe, May 17, 1933, NA RG 174, Entry 167/838, Box 183.

29. June 15, 1933, NA RG 174, Entry 167/838, Box 183.

30. Women's Bureau, "Gainful Employment of Married Women," 17.

31. "Resolution," The Texas Federation of Business and Professional Women, June 11, 1932, NA RG 174, Entry 167/838, Box 183. In the same file, see also a resolution from the Government Workers' Council of the National Woman's Party, March 7, 1933, demanding the removal of section 232 from the National Economy Act "as soon as the 73rd Congress convenes." On July 13, 1932, Secretary of Labor William Doak replied to a similar resolution: "It is my endeavor to administer the Economy Bill in such a way that no discharges will be necessary. You can be assured that full justice will be rendered to all women employees, married or unmarried." NA RG 174, Entry 167/838, Box 183.

32. Mrs. C.C. Beach to Frances Perkins, April 27, 1933, NA RG 174, Entry 167/838, Box 183.

33. The empirical work of Judith Buber Agassi, which explores worker attitudes in the 1970s, indicates that the stance still prevails: *Comparing the Work Attitudes of Women and Men* (Lexington, Mass.: D.C. Heath, 1982), especially chap. 5 and 10.

34. William Einger of Cincinnati, Ohio, to FDR, April 9, 1933, NA RG 174, Entry 167/838, Box 183. For a striking example of conflicted feelings among married men about single men holding jobs while those with families were unemployed, see the testimony of Frank Davidson, re: The Fisher Body Company. "There was one time in 1932 the company asked for them to bring their marriage certificates when they got a job and was hired for proof whether they were married or whether they were single. I know of cases where they went out and borrowed somebody else's marriage certificates. It is an awful stirred up mess, everything mixed up" (National Recovery Administration, *Hearings on Regularizing Employment and Otherwise Improving the Conditions of Labor in the Automobile Industry*, Flint, Mich., December 18, 1934, typescript in NA RG 9, Entry 44, Box 7265, 482). See also

testimony of M.R. Egbert, in Ibid., Milwaukee, Wis., December 30, 1934, Box 7266, 136.

35. Mary Winslow, *Married Women in Industry,* Women's Bureau Bulletin no. 38 (Washington, D.C.: Government Printing Office, 1924), 6.

36. Tamara Hareven, *Family Time and Industrial Time: The Relationship between Family and Work in a New England Community* (Cambridge, England: Cambridge University Press, 1982), 78; Jacquelyn Dowd Hall et al., *Like a Family: The Making of a Southern Cotton Mill World* (Chapel Hill: University of North Carolina Press, 1987), chap. 2.

37. Miss Thelma Pontney to FDR, June 30, 1933, NA RG 174, Entry 167/838, Box 183.

38. Miss Clara Rossberg of St. Paul, Minn., to FDR, May 18, 1933, NA RG 174, Entry 107/838, Box 183.

39. Mrs. C.M. Rogers to FDR, April 4, 1933, in ibid. Her position was echoed by Adele Simmonds of Chester, Pa., who wrote to Frances Perkins on behalf of her daughter (May 15, 1933): "I take on myself the pleasure of having a heart to heart talk with you concerning the idea of married women holding positions and single girls whose parents have denied themselves so much . . . fail to find jobs. . . . I do hope," she concluded, "for the good of our young generation there will soon be a law where married women will be illimenated from schools and offices. A single girl can't even get a position in a store because they are all taken up with married women."

40. Ankron to FDR, March 21, 1933, in ibid.

41. Mrs. Georgia Ervin of Columbus, Ga., to FDR, August 8, 1933, NA RG 9, Entry 398, Box 5, File: Bibb Manufacturing Co.

42. Jno Brogan of Pittsburgh, Pa., to Frances Perkins, July 12, 1933. And see M.B. Henley to the president, May 18, 1933. She is a single woman from Rossville, Ga., who castigated the "reconstruction army" for accepting "young single men who do not *need* the money they would get," while rejecting "young married men with families . . . willing to send their money home to help take care of their wives and children," both in NA RG 174, Entry 167/838, Box 183.

43. L.A. Cook to Gen. Hugh Johnson, March 7, 1934, NA RG 9, Entry 398, Box 8, File: Cannon Mills, Plant No. 6, Concord, N.C. Written in pencil on lined paper. Compare also, W.K. Valley to Hugh Johnson in the same file. Workers in Flint, Mich., echoed the complaint that their employers had brought in farmers in order to "lay the old men off and keep wages down" (Hearings, Flint, Mich., December 18, 1934, 572, 582).

44. Mrs. Lee A. Crayton to NRA, February 16, 1934. See also S.J. Gwynn to Hugh Johnson, June 7, 1934. Both in NA RG 9, Entry 398, Box 8, File: Cannon Mills, Plant No. 6, Concord, N.C.; and see as well Mr. and Mrs. P. J. Rookes to Hugh Johnson, March 9, 1934, NA RG 9, Entry 398, Box 3, File: Arnall Mills, Sargeant, Ga.

45. R.A. Gailey of Monitor, Wash., to Gen. Hugh Johnson, August 9, 1933, NA RG 9, Entry 23, PI 44, Box 491.

46. Sam Raspy of Anderson, Ind., to FDR, May 21, 1933, NA RG 174, Entry 167/838, Box 183.

47. Mr. R.D. Nio, Jr., to FDR, February 2, 1935, NA RG 9, Entry 23, Box 491. The tone of many letters indicated their refusal to believe that there might be another sense of justice. For example, Sarah M. Jones of Winsted, Conn., to FDR, April 25, 1933, NA RG 174, Entry 167/838, Box 183, asked why married women were "*allowed* to work in factories." And Earl Leiby protested "the fact that married women are *permitted* to work" at all. Glenn Purdy of Tulsa, Okla., to FDR, April 18, 1933, in ibid., argued that "no married woman has *any right* to command a salary when her husband is employed. . . . if you would bring prosperity back to our country, put married women by legislation out of the jobs which *rightfully* belong to men and unmarried women" (emphasis in these quotes mine).

48. Frank Dale to Hugh Johnson, September 21, 1933, NA RG 9, Entry 23, Box 491.

49. Rogers to FDR, April 4, 1933, in ibid.

50. Joseph Gildard to FDR, January 31, 1935, NA RG 9, Entry 23, Box 491.

51. Miss E. Blanche Evans, of Topeka, Kans., to FDR, May 9, 1933. And see as well F. J. Moeckly to FDR, August 11, 1933. Both in NA RG 174, Entry 167/838, Box 183. The latter, a male, identified himself as the president of the People's Economic and Social Welfare Association, and asserted that the President should "issue a proclamation asking public officials and private enterprises to eliminate duplication [of incomes] . . . in order to give employment to those who are a public charge."

52. Frances S. Key-Smith of Washington, D.C., to Vice-President Charles Curtis, November 12, 1931, NA RG 174, Entry 167/838, Box 183. He is a lawyer.

53. L.W. Taylor of Atlanta, Ga., to FDR, April 4, 1933, in ibid. He identifies himself as a disabled American veteran.

54. Miss Winifred Murray of Syracuse, N.Y., to FDR, July 18, 1933, in ibid.

55. Henley to FDR, May 18, 1933. See also Lola E. Painter of Cincinnati, Ohio, to Frances Perkins, April 26, 1933, in ibid., who told the story of how she had confronted a married woman at her job. It was, she wrote, "so pitiful at night to walk down [Main Street] and see lovely young women trying to sell their body for enough to pay room rent and get something to eat. So I said to this woman: do you ever go down Main St. near midnight. She said: certainly not, no self-respecting *decent* woman would and *I* said, and yet women like you put so many of them on Main St."

56. Murray to FDR, July 18, 1933.

57. Mrs. Beatrice Hobart Steely of Beverly Hills, Calif., to FDR, May 5, 1933, NA RG 174, Entry 167/838, Box 183.

58. John P. Holley to FDR, March 10, 1933, ibid.

59. Sam Raspy to FDR, May 21, 1933.

60. A.H. Davenport of Tampa, Fla., to FDR, May 22, 1933, NA RG 174, Entry 167/838, Box 183. The historical roots of this sense of justice about the purpose of a wage clearly go back some distance, as is indicated by the following quote from a group of Harrisburg, Penn., employees of the Pennsylvania Railroad during World War I. Women, they claimed, "spend all they make on their backs, while hard working men sacrificed their personal desires for the greater welfare of their families" (Maurine Greenwald, *Women, War and Work: The Impact of World War I on Women Workers in the United States* [Westport, Conn.: Greenwood Press, 1980], 131).

61. Frances S. Key-Smith to Charles Curtis, November 12, 1931.

62. Rossberg to FDR, May 18, 1933.

63. Steely to FDR, May 5, 1933. Steely went on to say, "And I, a woman of fifty, am forced to do menial work to keep from starving, largely because some married woman is holding a position I could occupy with equal efficiency." And see also Murray to FDR, July 19, 1933, who complained that "many of the married women so employed use the money derived therefrom for personal luxuries, while the same amount of money, or possibly less, would be used for food, clothes and shelter for some unemployed single girl with perhaps no home or parents."

64. Forbush to Wanda Dabkowski, April 10, 1934, NA RG 9, Entry 23, Box 491.

4. THE DOUBLE MEANING OF EQUAL PAY

1. From an American Federation of Labor resolution quoted by Elizabeth J. Hauser, "Women Workers and the Trade Union Movement," *American Federationist*, 17 (April 1910), 305.

2. For example, the bill replaced the word *comparable* with *equal* and added the conditions of effort, responsibility, and working conditions. It took the form of an amendment to the Fair Labor Standards Act of 1938, which reduced coverage to those included within the scope of the FLSA. I have cited the text of the bill from the Report of the House Committee on Education and Labor, May 20, 1963, as reprinted in the Bureau of National Affairs, *Equal Pay for Equal Work* (Washington, D.C.: Bureau of National Affairs, 1963), 93, 98.

3. Cynthia Harrison, *On Account of Sex: The Politics of Women's Issues, 1945-1968* (Berkeley: University of California Press, 1988), 96, 99. Harrison contains an excellent description of the political process of passing the bill.

4. "Equal Pay for Women," *American Federationist*, 71 (July 1964), 14.

5. "When Women Get Paid as Much as Men," *U.S. News and World Report*, June 3, 1963, 97.

6. Thomas P. Nelson, "Bill to Assure Women 'Equal Pay' Alarms Employers' Lobbyists," *Wall Street Journal*, August 10, 1962, 1.

7. Michelle Barrett and Mary McIntosh, "The 'Family Wage': Some Problems for Socialists and Feminists," *Capital and Class*, 11 (1980), 52.

8. For example, see Mary Blewett, *Men, Women and Work: Class, Gender and Protest in the New England Shoe Industry, 1780-1910* (Urbana: University of Illinois Press, 1988), 175, 283.

9. Bureau of National Affairs, *Equal Pay for Equal Work*, 3; see also Luke Grant, "Women in Trade Unions," *American Federationist*, 10 (August 1903), 656.

10. U.S. Department of Labor, Women's Bureau, *"Equal Pay" for Women in War Industries*, Bulletin no. 196 (Washington, D.C.: Government Printing Office, 1942), 17; Bureau of National Affairs, *Equal Pay for Equal Work*, 3; Valerie Conner, "'The Mothers of the Race' in World War I: The National War Labor Board and Women in Industry," *Labor History*, 21 (Winter 1979/80), 51. And see also "Women and Wages," *Woman Citizen*, June 17, 1919, 8, which reports that a Massachusetts union that admitted women to membership during the war concluded that "finding that employers began at once to exploit women

by paying them as small a wage as was possible, the men have now decided to demand equal pay for equal work."

11. Olga S. Halsey to Mary Van Kleeck, typescript memo entitled "Equal Pay for Equal Work," July 8, 1918, National Archives, Record Group 86: Records of the Women's Bureau, Box 385, File: Equal Pay, 1918. (Hereinafter referred to as NA RG 86.)

12. But this was by no means exclusive. For example, Haverhill shoe stitchers (female) included a demand for equal pay in the 1895 shoe workers' strike, which seems to have been for the purpose of fostering female independence rather than fending off male complaints of competition. See Blewett, *Men, Women and Work*, 283.

13. See Lynn Weiner, *From Working Girl to Working Mother: The Female Labor Force in the United States, 1820-1980* (Chapel Hill: University of North Carolina, 1985), chap. 2, for a summary of increases around the turn of the century. The figures were greater in large cities. According to Joanne Meyerowitz, *Women Adrift: Independent Wage Earners in Chicago, 1880-1930* (Chicago: University of Chicago Press, 1988), 5, between 1880 and 1930, Chicago's female labor force increased by 1,000 percent, or three times the rate of women in the labor force as a whole.

14. Grant, "Women in Trade Unions," 656.

15. Hauser, "Women Workers and the Trade Union Movement," 306.

16. Florence Thorne, "Women and War Service," *American Federationist*, 24 (June 1917), 455; during the war Gompers added the demand for equal pay to several demands to regulate women's entry into the labor force. See, for example, the editorials entitled, "Women Workers in War Times," *American Federationist*, 24 (September 1917), 747; and "Don't Sacrifice Womanhood," in ibid., 24 (August 1917), 640. For prewar statements about equal pay, see Melinda Scott, "The Way to Freedom," in ibid., 22 (September 1915), 731. Maurine Greenwald, *Women, War and Work: The Impact of World War I on Women Workers in the United States* (Westport, Conn.: Greenwood Press, 1980), 128-38, 177-80, notes that these boundaries were not permanently crossed.

17. Cited in typescript from "Women's Work and War," 1 (July 1918), 3, in NA RG 86, Box 385, File: Equal Pay, 1918.

18. "The Government and Women in Industry," *American Federationist*, 25 (September 1918), 788.

19. Elizabeth Anne Payne, *Reform, Labor and Feminism: Margaret Dreier Robins and the Women's Trade Union League* (Urbana: Universi-

ty of Illinois Press, 1988), 129.

20. Arthur Ross, *Trade Union Wage Policy* (Berkeley: University of California Press, 1953 [1948]), 46-64, chap. 5.

21. Typescript, "Equal Pay Examples (Equal or Unequal)," in NA RG 86, Box 385, File: Equal Pay, 1918.

22. "Women Workers Organize to Win," *American Federationist*, 23 (March 1916), 200.

23. Thorne, "Women and War Service," 455.

24. See Ronald Schatz, *The Electrical Workers: A History of Labor at General Electric and Westinghouse, 1923-60* (Urbana: University of Illinois Press, 1983), 126, 172, for a discussion of these issues.

25. Testimony of John Bartee, NRA *Hearings on Regularizing Employment and Otherwise Improving the Conditions of Labor in the Automobile Industry*, South Bend, Ind; January 2, 1935, National Archives, Record Group 9, Records of the National Recovery Administration, Entry 44, Box 7266. (Hereinafter referred to as NA RG 9.)

26. Maud Younger to Hugh Johnson, October 28, 1933, NA RG 9, Entry 23, Box 489.

27. Typescript of Introduction to Bulletin 152, NA RG 86, Box 385, Files Regarding Equal Pay, File: Equal Pay, 1935.

28. Ruth Milkman, *Gender at Work: The Dynamics of Job Segregation by Sex during World War II* (Urbana: University of Illinois Press, 1987); Ruth Roach Pierson, *"They're Still Women After All: The Second World War and Canadian Womanhood* (Toronto: McClelland and Stuart, 1986); Karen Anderson, *Wartime Women: Sex Roles, Family Relations, and the Status of Women during World War II* (Westport, Conn.: Greenwood Press, 1981).

29. Anna Weitzel to Bertha Nienburg, January 16, 1943, NA RG 86, Box 385, File: Equal Pay, 1943.

30. Mrs. Anna Matson of Sioux City, Iowa, to FDR, May 14, 1943, NA RG 86, Box 385, File: Equal Pay, 1943.

31. Mrs. Gertrude Coburn, of Alliance, Ohio, to Frances Perkins, August 28, 1943, NA RG 86, Box 385, File: Equal Pay, 1943.

32. Mrs. Adeline Hering to FDR, June 23, 1943, NA RG 86, Box 385, File: Equal Pay, 1943.

33. Nora Galloway to FDR, September 29, 1942, NA RG 86, Box 385, File: Equal Pay, 1942.

34. Ethel Lee to Mary Anderson, undated, NA RG 86, Box 385, File: Equal Pay, 1944.

35. Typescript headed, "Equal Pay Section of Statement dictated

by Mary Anderson for War History of Women's Bureau; then revised by Rachel F. Nyswander after consulting official files and conferring with Miss Nienburg," NA RG 86, Box 385, File: Equal Pay, 1945, 2.

36. William H. Davis to Frances Perkins, June 4, 1943, NA RG 86, Box 385, File: Equal Pay, 1943.

37. Typescript of excerpts from Helen Baker, "Wage Rates and Wage Policies," in NA RG 86, Box 385, File: Equal Pay, 1942.

38. NA RG 86, Box 251, File: Wage Determination—Notes, Case no. 8.

39. Typescript of a talk by A.L. Kress, "Equal Pay for Equal Work," in NA RG 86, Box 385, File: Equal Pay, 1943.

40. Z. Clark Dickinson, "Men's and Women's Wages in the United States," *International Labour Review*, 47 (June 1943), 711.

41. Typescript, "Importance to Postwar American Economic Objectives of Equal Pay for Women and Men and the Raising of Substandard Wages of Women," July 9, 1945, NA RG 86, Box 385, File: Equal Pay, July 1945. The memo was apparently prepared in an effort to persuade the War Labor Board (which had long acknowledged the weight of community tradition in setting wages for gender-differentiated jobs) to alter its policies.

42. *Christian Science Monitor*, Magazine section, April 13, 1946; found in NA RG 86, Box 390; File: Equal Pay, News Clippings. Note that this comes close to, but does not quite reach, today's conception of comparable worth in that it called for comparing only jobs that were similar, not those that required similar skill, effort, and responsibility.

43. Wage Determination Hearings, NA RG 86, Box 252, File: Alden's Incorporated.

44. Wage Determination Hearings, NA RG 86, Box 253, File: Singer Manufacturing Co., 7.

45. Wage Determination Hearings, NA RG 86, Box 252, File: Dowst Manufacturing Co., 6.

46. Typescript, "Equal Pay," July 18, 1949, NA RG 86, Box 385, File: Equal Pay, 1949.

47. Ibid., 3.

48. Ibid.

49. "Hearings before a Sub-committee of the Committee of Education and Labor on S1178," U.S. Senate, Seventy-ninth Congress, First session, October 29, 30, 31, 1945, 12. (Hereinafter referred to as Equal Pay Hearings, 1945.)

50. Frances Whitlock to Miss Miller, August 22, 1945, NA RG 86, Box 389, File: Equal Pay, 1945.

51. The number increased to twenty-two by 1963. Bureau of National Affairs, *Equal Pay for Equal Work*, 31; the remaining states included California, Connecticut, Minnesota, New Jersey, Arkansas, Colorado, and Oregon, in addition to Michigan and Montana, both of which had passed legislation in 1919.

52. A 1956 study of 510 union contracts found 195 (38 percent) included equal pay clauses. A 1961 study concluded that only 18 percent had such clauses. These were most prevalent in textile, electrical and nonelectrical machinery, food and transportation equipment. Bureau of National Affairs, *Equal Pay for Equal Work*, 5.

53. This history is chronicled in Harrison, *On Account of Sex*, chap. 3, 6.

54. Typescripts, "Equal Pay for Women Industrial Workers in the United States" and "Economic Desirability of Equal Pay," in NA RG 86, Box 385, File: Equal Pay, 1942.

55. Helen Baker, typescripts of extracts from "Wage Rates and Wage Policies," *Women in War Industries* (Princeton: Princeton University Press, 1942), found in NA RG 86, Box 385, File: Equal Pay, 1943.

56. Frieda S. Miller to Mr. Sherman, Assistant Solicitor, July 20 1945, NA RG 86, Box 385, File: Equal Pay, July 1945.

57. Typescript, "Movement for Equal Pay Legislation in the United States," March 17, 1949, NA RG 86, Box 385, File: Equal Pay, 1949.

58. Congressional Record, May 17, 1963, vol. 109, part 7, 8914.

59. George Addes to regional directors of the UAW, June 10, 1943, RG 86, Box 385, File: Equal Pay, 1943.

60. Testimony of Lewis Schwellenbach, Hearings, 1945, 5.

61. Testimony of Elizabeth Christman, "Hearings before Subcommittee no. 4 of the Committee on Education and Labor," House of Representatives, Eightieth Congress, Second session, February 9, 10, 11, and 13, 1948, 68. (Hereinafter referred to as Equal Pay Hearings, 1948.)

62. Testimony of Helen Moore, an employee of Fisher Body Co., member of local 602, UAW-CIO, Lansing, Mich., Equal Pay Hearings, 1948, 182; Testimony of Hartman Barber, General Representative, Brotherhood of Railway and Steamship Clerks, Equal Pay Hearings, 1948, 157.

63. Ibid., 213.

64. Testimony of Frieda Miller, Equal Pay Hearings, 1945, 16.

65. Testimony of Lewis Schwellenbach, Equal Pay Hearings, 1945, 5-6; and compare 131-32.

66. Christman, Equal Pay Hearings, 1945, 106; see also testimony of Helen Gahagan Douglas, Equal Pay Hearings, 1948, 12; as well as the comment of Lewis Schwellenbach: "There is no sex differential in the food she buys or the rent she pays. There should be none in her pay envelope. I still believe in the truth of the old adage . . . that 'the laborer is worthy of his hire'" (Equal Pay Hearings, 1948, 83). The comment was frequently echoed in the 1963 debates that led to the passage of the Equal Pay Act of 1963. See, for example, the comments of Representative Sickles and Senators Hart and McDowell, in Committee on Education and Labor, House of Representatives, Eighty-eighth Congress, First session, "Legislative History of the Equal Pay Act of 1963," 65, 55, and 70.

67. Statement of Helen Moore, an employee of Fisher Body Co.; member of Local 602, UAW-CIO, Lansing, Mich., Equal Pay Hearings, 1948, 183.

68. Maurice J. Tobin, "Equal Pay—Present Reality of Future Dream," *Report of the National Conference on Equal Pay," March 31 and April 1, 1952*, Women's Bureau, Bulletin no. 243 (Washington, D.C.: Government Printing Office, 1952), 8.

69. Ibid.

70. Quoted in Bureau of National Affairs, *Equal Pay for Equal Work*, from the Senate Committee on Labor and Public Welfare, Report on S1909, May 17, 1963, 101.

71. Testimony of Frieda Miller, Equal Pay Hearings, 1945, 17.

72. Statement of the League of Women Shoppers, Inc., N.Y., Equal Pay Hearings, 1945, 111.

73. Statement of Lewis G. Hines, Equal Pay Hearings, 1945, 122; and see testimony of Frieda Miller, Equal Pay Hearings, 1948, 155.

74. Testimony of Frieda Miller, Equal Pay Hearings, 1945, 17.

75. Testimony of Lewis Schwellenbach, Equal Pay Hearings, 1945, 6.

76. Tobin, "Equal Pay," 9.

77. Testimony of Lewis Schwellenbach, Equal Pay Hearings, 1948, 77-78. Schwellenbach continued: "At a time when the mobility of labor is not so important in maintaining a healthy economy, and when full production is so essential in keeping the forces of inflation under control, I believe it is a duty of the Federal Government to take sound action to remove such deterrents to our economic health." And see also, Equal Pay Hearings, 1945, 110.

78. "Legislative History of the Equal Pay Act," 33-34; see also the comments of Rep. Ralph J. Rivers of Alaska, 63.

79. Equal Pay Hearings, 1945, 7.

80. "Legislative History of the Equal Pay Act," 29.

81. National Conference on Equal Pay, "Report of Committee on Findings," NA RG 86, Box 385, File: Equal Pay Hearings, 1952, p. 2.

82. "Legislative History of the Equal Pay Act," 29, 63.

83. Equal Pay Hearings, 1945, 11.

84. Arthur S. Fleming, "Keynote Address," *Report of the National Conference on Equal Pay, March 31 and April 1, 1952*, Women's Bureau, Bulletin no. 243 (Washington, D.C.: Government Printing Office, 1952), 13.

85. Arthur S. Fleming, "Equal Pay for Equal Work Is Simple Justice," *Good Housekeeping*, November 1962, 54.

86. "Legislative History of the Equal Pay Act," 63; Congressional Record, May 23, 1963, vol. 109, p. 7, 8692.

87. Testimony of Chase Going Woodhouse, Equal Pay Hearings, vol. 109, p. 7, 1945, 154.

88. Comments of Sen. McDowell, Congressional Record, May 23, 1963, 8752; "Legislative History of the Equal Pay Act," 70.

89. Quoted in the Bureau of National Affairs, *Equal Pay for Equal Work*, 109, from Congressional Record, May 22, 1963, 8683, 8684.

90. William Schnitzler, "Why Less Pay for Women Workers?" *The Bakers and Confectioners Journal*, 65 (March 1950), 12.

91. Testimony of William Miller, quoted in Bureau of National Affairs, *Equal Pay for Equal Work*, 54.

92. Equal Pay Hearings, 1948, 67.

93. Pennsylvania Salt Company, May 22, 1947, in NA RG 86, Box 251, File: Wage Determination—White Collar.

94. Testimony of William Miller in Bureau of National Affairs, "Legislative History of the Equal Pay Act," 54. This position is explored in Dickinson, "Men's and Women's Wages in the United States," 714-15.

95. Ibid., 56-59.

96. "Legislative History of the Equal Pay Act," 51.

97. Tobin, "Equal Pay," 7.

98. National Manpower Council, *Womanpower* (New York: Columbia University Press, 1957), 345.

99. All sides seem to have understood this. Note that as early as 1952, the National Conference on Equal Pay concluded that "attainment of equal pay would be a very limited victory unless women also

obtain equal job opportunities." (21). See also Esther Peterson's comment on the issue in Harrison, *On Account of Sex*, 100.

5. THE JUST PRICE

This chapter originated as the keynote address to the seventh Berkshire Conference on the History of Women, June 1987. It is reprinted from *Feminist Studies*, 14, no. 2 (Summer 1988), 235-50, by permission of the publisher, Feminist Studies, Inc., c/o Women's Studies Program, University of Maryland, College Park, Maryland, 20742.

1. Judith Rollins, *Between Women: Domestics and Their Employers* (Philadelphia: Temple University Press, 1985), 74.

2. *Brief of the American Civil Liberties Union et al., amici curiae, in California Federal Savings and Loan Association* v. *Mark Guerra*, No. 85-494, U.S. Supreme Court, 12-14; and *Brief of Equal Rights Advocates et al., amici curiae, in California Federal Savings and Loan Association* v. *Mark Guerra*, No. 85-494, U.S. Supreme Court, 7-9.

3. In *U.S. Steelworkers* v. *Weber*, 443 U.S. 193 (1979), the Supreme Court sustained a voluntary and temporary affirmative action plan to redress past grievances suffered by a specific group. Quotations are from the decision as it appeared in the *Daily Labor Report*, March 20, 1987, D 16.

4. "Comparable Worth: An Interview with Heidi Hartmann and June O'Neill," *New Perspectives*, 17 (September 1985), 29.

5. Donald J. Treiman and Heidi Hartmann, eds., *Women, Work, and Wages: Equal Pay for Jobs of Equal Value* (Washington, D.C.: National Academy Press, 1981), 28.

6. Ibid., ix.

7. Barbara R. Bergmann, "Pay Equity—Surprising Answers to Hard Questions," *Challenge*, 30 (May/June 1987), 47. See also Helen Remick, ed., *Comparable Worth and Wage Discrimination: Technical Possibilities and Political Realities* (Philadelphia: Temple University Press, 1984), for essays that are generally favorable to comparable worth.

8. Michael Levin, "Comparable Worth: The Feminist Road to Socialism," *Commentary*, 79 (September 1984), 13-19. See also E. Robert Livernash, ed., *Comparable Worth: Issues and Alternatives* (Washington, D.C.: Equal Employment Advisory Council, 1984), for essays that are generally opposed to comparable worth.

9. Raymond de Roover, "The Concept of the Just Price: Theory

and Economic Policy," in James Gherity, ed., *Economic Thought: A Historical Anthology* (New York: Random House, 1969), 23.

10. John Dunlop, "Wage Contours," in Michael Piore, ed., *Unemployment and Inflation: Institutional and Structural Views* (White Plains, N.Y.: M.E. Sharpe, 1979), 66. Elaine Sorenson, "Equal Pay for Comparable Worth: A Policy for Eliminating the Undervaluation of Women's Work," *Journal of Economic Issues,* 18 (June 1984), 465-72, provides a convenient summary of some of these arguments.

11. Arthur M. Ross, *Trade Union Wage Policy* (Berkeley: University of California Press, 1948), 49. See also Robert Solow, "Theories of Unemployment," *American Economic Review,* 70 (March 1980), 1-11.

12. Ross, *Trade Union Wage Policy,* 50-51 (emphasis mine).

13. Michael J. Piore, "Unemployment and Inflation: An Alternative View," in Piore, *Unemployment and Inflation,* 6. And see Peter Doeringer and Michael Piore, *Internal Labor Markets and Manpower Analysis* (Lexington, Mass.: Lexington Books, 1971).

14. Eileen Power, *Medieval Women* (London: Cambridge University Press, 1975), 60.

15. William Bielby and James Baron, "Undoing Discrimination: Job Integration and Comparable Worth," in Christine Bose and Glenna Spitz, eds., *Ingredients for Women's Employment Policy* (Albany: SUNY Press, 1987), 218.

16. "Corporate Women: They're about to Break through to the Top," *Business Week,* June 22, 1987, 74.

17. Edward Hallett Carr, *What Is History?* (New York: Knopf, 1962), 105-6.

18. Quoted in Mary Heen, "A Review of Federal Court Decisions under Title VII of the Civil Rights Act of 1964," in Remick, *Comparable Worth and Wage Discrimination,* 217.

19. See Ruth Milkman, "Women's History Goes to Trial," *Feminist Studies,* 12 (Summer 1986), 375-400; and Alice Kessler-Harris, "Equal Employment Opportunity Commission v. Sears Roebuck and Company: A Personal Account," *Radical History Review,* 35 (April 1986), 57-79.

20. Judith Long Laws, "Work Aspirations of Women: False Leads and New Starts," in Martha Blaxall and Barbara Reagan, *Women and the Workplace: The Implications of Occupational Segregation* (Chicago: University of Chicago Press, 1976), 33-49.

21. Carole Turbin, "Reconceptualizing Family, Work and Labor Organizing: Working Women in Troy, 1860-90," *Review of Radical*

Political Economy, 16 (Spring 1984), 1-16; Mary Blewett, *Men, Women, Work and Gender* (Champaign: University of Illinois Press, 1988).

22. Audre Lorde, "The Master's Tools Will Never Dismantle the Master's House," in Cherrie Moraga and Gloria Anzaldua, eds., *This Bridge Called My Back: Writings by Radical Women of Color* (New York: Kitchen Table Women of Color Press, 1983), 99.

23. Lillian Breslow Rubin, *Worlds of Pain: Life in the Working Class Family* (New York: Basic Books, 1976), 176.

24. Brigitte Berger and Peter L. Berger, *The War over the Family: Capturing the Middle Ground* (Garden City, N.Y.: Anchor Press, Doubleday, 1983), 205.

Index